The Servant Leader

Also by James A. Autry

Books

The Spirit of Retirement
Love and Profit: The Art of Caring Leadership
Life & Work: A Manager's Search for Meaning
Confessions of an Accidental Businessman
Real Power: Business Lessons from the Tao Te Ching (with
Stephen Mitchell)
Nights Under a Tin Roof (poetry)
Life After Mississippi (poetry)

Videos

Love & Profit
Life & Work
Spirit at Work
(Available from Star Thrower at 1-800-242-3220
or www.starthrower.com)

Praise for *The Servant Leader*

"Servant leadership is key to surviving and thriving in the twenty-first century. Let both Jim Autry and his book *The Servant Leader* be your guide."

—KEN BLANCHARD, COAUTHOR OF *The One Minute Manager*

"*The Servant Leader* describes the kind of leadership upon which Starbucks Coffee Company has been built, and is a concept that is closely aligned with our mission and guiding principles. Starbucks partners (employees) are focused on being of service to each other, the communities where they operate, and to each customer one cup at a time."

—HOWARD SCHULTZ, CHAIRMAN, STARBUCKS

"*The Servant Leader* illuminates a clear path to personal, spiritual, and material actualization, which, in return, creates an infinite circle of prosperity."

—TOM GOULD, RETIRED CHAIRMAN AND CEO,
YOUNKERS, INC.

"Quite simply, this is an extraordinary book. For those yet unfamiliar with the principles and concepts of servant leadership, *The Servant Leader* will provide the ideal introduction. For those who have been working with and trying to promote servant leadership in their own organizations, it will very quickly become their ultimate book of reference. From principles and practicalities, it is a classic already and the first truly great leadership book of the new century."

—JOHN NOBLE, DIRECTOR, GREENLEAF CENTER, UK

"With a business environment where increasing change is the only constant, Jim Autry, one of the true pioneers in leadership, offers through *The Servant Leader* an abundant buffet of insightful, practical suggestions on how to heartfully create better business results. *The Servant Leader* is really the best field guide I've seen for helping managers transform themselves into true leaders." —DOUG GREENE, CEO, NEW HOPE GROUP

"A much needed addition to the servant leadership movement!"
—JAMES C. HUNTER, AUTHOR OF *The World's Most Powerful Leadership Principle* AND *The Servant*

"Jim Autry continues to chronicle the leader journey in clear, wise, and witty prose and poems. I love his dedication and vivid expression of the essential character and skills of today's leaders. He is telling the truth—I urge you to listen to him."
—MARGARET J. WHEATLEY, AUTHOR OF *Leadership and the New Science*

"Jim Autry combines a deep compassion for the human condition and a yearning for people to live the richest personal and professional lives, with a rigorous and logical approach to optimizing business performance. His courage in broaching the issues which get in the way of the latter but which can so easily be dismissed as "non-business" or "touchy-feely" issues are a true integration of spiritual and business matters.
—MATT HANDBURY, EXECUTIVE CHAIRMAN, MURDOCH MAGAZINES

THE SERVANT LEADER

How to Build a Creative
Team, Develop Great
Morale, and Improve
Bottom-Line Performance

JAMES A. AUTRY

 THREE RIVERS PRESS • NEW YORK

To Lieutenant Governor Sally Pederson of Iowa,
who is not only the most caring servant leader
I know but also my best friend and my wife.

Published by Three Rivers Press, New York, New York.
Member of the Crown Publishing Group, a division of Random House, Inc.
www.randomhouse.com

Originally published in hardcover by Prima Publishing in 2001.

THREE RIVERS PRESS and the Tugboat design are registered trademarks of Random House, Inc.

Printed in the United States of America

Library of Congress Cataloging-in-Publication Data
Autry, James A.
   The servant leader : how to build a creative team, develop great morale, and improve bottom-line performance/ James A. Autry
   Includes index.
   1. Leadership. I. Title.
BF637.L4 A88   2001
158′.4—dc21   2001033933

ISBN 1-4000-5473-7

10 9 8 7 6 5 4 3

First Paperback Edition

Contents

Acknowledgments

IF ANYONE DESERVES the lion's share of credit for the creation of this book it is my editor, Alice Feinstein. She virtually talked me into writing it, a rare thing indeed in the concourse between editor and author. From her initial e-mail and subsequent phone calls has developed one of the most satisfying professional relationships of my career. So I thank her for that as well as specifically for this book.

I can't name all the people who have been important to my journey as businessman, author, and consultant, thus to the writing of *The Servant Leader*, so I'll just say that I have been blessed with role models and mentors and teachers and friends throughout my several careers. And in a way, everything I write has been borne of those relationships.

Foreword

by Howard Behar

I AM SINCERELY GRATEFUL to have been asked to share my thoughts about *The Servant Leader*. From the first time I encountered his work, Jim Autry's writing has helped to crystallize and give voice to many of the leadership principles that instinctively felt like the right thing to do, but I hadn't yet found a way to articulate.

Nearly thirty years ago, I was introduced to the concept of servant leadership through Robert Greenleaf's pamphlet on the subject. I pored over the text again and again to glean the information I needed to truly become a better leader in my heart and my daily life. It was Jim Autry who eventually brought the information to life for me and many others.

When I first read Jim's work, I was thrilled. Finally, someone had clearly and concisely articulated these principles in a way that people can quickly adopt into their lives. The impact is huge—when hundreds of people in an organization are participating in a change process, they need to be able to quickly absorb the basic concepts and get down to the business of making it real. I've seen it happen.

Since 1989, I've had the great pleasure, frustration, joy, and challenge of being part of the Starbucks organization. When I joined Starbucks, the company had just expanded from Seattle (our hometown) to Chicago, and it was a huge stretch. No one was sure that the concept would work outside the Pacific Northwest. We were feverishly working to bring the *Starbucks Experience* to people across the country. Everyone at Starbucks, including Chairman Howard Schultz and I, had lots of intense, soul-searching, and sometimes animated (read: loud!) conversations about how we could nurture the company and continue to grow. We argued over everything from the color of the napkins to offering non-fat milk to our customers.

But we never had a disagreement about our principles, our values, and our mission as an organization. We had high aspirations, but they weren't just about making money. Sure, you have to make a profit to keep your business going and it's nice to live a comfortable life, but that can't be the primary objective. There has to be some driving spirit behind your work, something that makes it authentic to everyone involved. In the early days of Starbucks we articulated our ideals in our Mission Statement and Guiding Principles. We remain passionately committed to those principles. Partners (Starbucks employees) are exposed to our ideals in the interview process and throughout their careers—they dominate our decision making and daily work. And now, many years after those early conversations, Starbucks is a global organization which has enjoyed tremendous success on a variety of fronts. And we believe that the best is yet to come.

The pathway of Starbucks' phenomenal achievement has been full of twists and hurdles, some of which were unwittingly created by the very partners who were working so hard to make us successful! I retired from Starbucks in 1999, and was enjoying the good life—no meetings, no deadlines—it was great. But in 2001 there was a change in the leadership in our Retail North America business unit, and Starbucks President and Chief Executive Officer Orin Smith asked me to come back to work on an interim basis as president of the business unit.

Orin had noticed something different at Starbucks. The passion and values were still there, but sometimes we spent more energy on our individual or department goals than focusing on the greater good. Not just what we could do within the four walls of our offices or stores, but the greater good that our now-expansive organization was bringing to the world—how we could serve each other and people around the globe. From an outsiders' perspective, there was nothing to complain about: the company's financial achievements, growth and innovation were chugging ahead full steam, and partners devoted near-obsessive attention to quality and ethics. (Starbucks partners are some of the most caring and highly motivated people you'll ever meet.) But could we sustain our success for the next 10, 20, 50 years without taking a hard look at our leadership practices? We didn't think so.

Orin and I began to evangelize the principles of servant leadership. We exposed people to Jim's writings in *The Servant Leader* and *Love and Profit,* and got them excited about learning more. One of the best moves we ever made was to invite Jim to come to Starbucks to personally introduce the concept of servant leadership to our senior management team. The rest is history. Jim's enthusiasm, energy and spirit had our partners hooked. They were enthralled by the concept of servant leadership; Jim made it real and vibrant and achievable.

Jim put a vocabulary and a structure to everything that we were thinking and feeling. He gave people the information and the permission they needed to truly become servant leaders. He gave us the right questions to ask ourselves and others. We were perfectly poised to take on the ideals of servant leadership and make them a reality every day. We held trainings, read books, and most importantly, we lived it. And we still are living it. You can see it today as people meet in the hallways. You can feel the power behind the change, and the power that servant leadership gives to everyone it touches, in every aspect of our lives. Servant leadership is truly alive and well at Starbucks.

One of the key principles that Jim advocates is that we have to have congruity in our lives. You can't separate the way you behave when you're communicating with your spouse from the way you communicate with your co-workers or boss. It's important to be the same person all day, every day. Over many years, and with a lot of struggle, I have been able to incorporate the ideals of Jim Autry's *The Servant Leader* into every aspect of my life—my marriage, my friendships, my work—the sum of who I am as a person.

I see the power that we each have to enhance each others' lives. Jim Autry's work helped bring that power to my life. Thanks, Jim.

Howard Behar
Retired President, Starbucks Coffee International
Director, Starbucks Corporation

Introduction

IN WORKING WITH A variety of managers and executives over the past several years, I've found myself facing the same three comments over and over: (1) "Our organization is very different from other organizations," or (2) "We feel that your ideas would take too much time; they're not efficient," or (3) "What you teach is the soft side of management, and that just doesn't work very well in an organization like ours."

When I hear these statements, I remain polite in my responses but really just want to say, "Nonsense."

I've been involved in the management of, have consulted for, and have counseled and coached the executives and employees of all kinds of organizations, for-profit and nonprofit, in this country; plus I have consulted and coached for ten years with a large company in Australia. I've led leadership workshops for the commanding general of the Air National Guard and his staff at the Pentagon, have addressed the conference of the adjutants general of all the states, have done values workshops for a state governor and his staff, have taught leadership skills to a mayor and his staff, have worked with universities, teacher groups, and labor unions. I've consulted with dotcom companies as well as manufacturing companies, agribusinesses, natural products companies, and media.

I say this not to brag, but to make the following points in response to the three comments that greet me almost everywhere I go:

1. Whoever you are, reader, your organization is not different. You may have a different product or a different mission, a different organizational structure, or a different management style. You may have a unique manufacturing process or distribution system, or, if you're a nonprofit, a special way of fund-raising or delivering services. You may have a lot of things that are different. But fundamentally, your organization is not different, because it depends on people, and it is that dependence on people that makes you and your organization far more similar to, than dissimilar from, your counterparts and their organizations elsewhere.

2. Efficiency is not the same as effectiveness, and a preoccupation with efficiency has proved, over and over again, to be the enemy of effectiveness. We need look no further than the American automobile industry of the sixties and seventies, where emphasis on efficiency at the expense of effectiveness allowed the Japanese auto industry to capture a devastating share of the market.

3. There is nothing "soft" or easy about the kind of leadership I try to teach, whether you call it caring leadership or servant leadership, but it works. It works in every kind of organization and with every kind of em-

ployee group. I know it works. I've seen it work. I've made it work. It will enhance productivity, encourage creativity, and benefit the bottom line. But it's not easy, and after reading this book, I think you'll agree. As I've said so many times, as a good-humored challenge, "If you think it's soft or easy, why don't you just give it a try and get back to me?"

Again, this is not to be arrogant but to express my strong belief that leadership, or management if you prefer, approached properly, is a calling. Not just a job but a calling. Think about it. As a manager, much of the psychological, emotional, and financial well-being of other people is dependent on you and on how well you create the circumstances and the environment in which they can do their jobs.

If indeed you feel these responsibilities deeply, if the people and their needs engage your own psychological and emotional energies, then I suggest that you already approach management as a calling. Let me suggest further that if you think of it as a calling in the service of the people for whom you are responsible, then you already have transcended the label "manager" and have become a leader.

Just as important, this kind of leadership will empower you to be the kind of *person* you want to be while being the kind of *leader* you want to be.

And let me emphasize this: *Leadership in service of others requires a great deal of courage.* It was far easier to be the old top-down kind of boss, but this book is not about easy answers. Just as business, or organizational life of any sort, is not about what's efficient, it's also not about what's easy. It's about what's most effective. And what we've learned is that over the long-term, the old top-down, command-control ways don't work as well as some managers would like to think. They dispirit and frustrate people; they suppress creativity; and they rob organizations of people's best efforts.

The military doesn't even do it the old way anymore, so it's all the more perplexing that so many managers in business want to hold on to old definitions of power. Could it be that a power trip is more enjoyable when you're able to flex your manager muscles a bit? (Hey, I'm feeling powerful today. Think I'll yell at somebody.)

Yet while there are servant leaders who are thought of as nice and easygoing, and there are those who undoubtedly are loved by their colleagues and employees, servant leadership is also not about being nice or being loved; nor is it about never having to do the gut-wrenching stuff like firing people. It is, however, a way of being that combines the personal characteristics outlined in chapter 1 with self-discipline and the unwavering commitment to creating a workplace of efficacy and productivity as well as of opportunity for personal and spiritual growth for all.

At the same time, it allows you, the leader, to grow personally and to find more meaning in your life and work, just as you are helping others grow. That's why I offer this book for your examination and, I hope, for your inspiration to become a servant leader.

While you're working to attain this way of being and leading, I hope you will depend on this book as a reference, but only until you are able to face these leadership challenges on your own, acting from your own center. At that point, pass the book along to someone else.

PART ONE

A Foundation of Character and Vision

TRUE LEADERSHIP, UNLIKE MANAGEMENT, is not just a set of skills and learned behaviors. What you do as a leader will depend on who you are. And regardless of your own perceptions of yourself, those around you in the workplace—colleagues and employees—can determine who you are only by observing what you do. They can't see inside your head, they can't know what you think or how you feel, they can't subliminally detect your compassion or pain or joy or goodwill. In other words, the only way you can manifest your character, your personhood, and your spirit in the workplace is through your behavior.

The subject of spirituality and work is increasing in popularity, and it is certainly one of the philosophical bases of servant leadership, but there is too often the tendency to think that "feeling spiritual" is all there is to it. Your practical, everyday challenge in organizational life is not to be a guru but to be a leader. And to paraphrase a very old expression, "Servant leadership is as servant leadership does."

So I begin this book with two chapters that focus on the subjects of being and behavior.

Chapter 1 addresses specifically the characteristics of servant leadership; the five ways of being that, if you can master them, will assure your growth and progress as a leader. Certain behaviors flow naturally from these characteristics, and it is through these behaviors that your people will be able to recognize and benefit from your leadership. I have attempted to give real-world examples that provide you with lessons you can apply to your own leadership situation.

Chapter 2 extends the subjects of being and behavior into an organizational framework to address the sometimes vague or slippery subject of vision. A primary function of the servant leader is to assure that an organization's people are imbued with a clear understanding of vision. Beyond that, the leader must help people relate that vision to their own vision in a way that directly aligns their work with the goals they want to accomplish and the goals of the organization.

It is upon the foundation of these two chapters—the being and behavior of the leader and the people of an organization—that the rest of the book has been developed.

CHAPTER ONE

Characteristics of the Leader as Servant

IN *THE CAINE MUTINY*, the vivid and complex World War II novel, Herman Wouk describes a destroyer as "a master plan designed by geniuses for execution by idiots." Wouk's description is a mite cynical and perhaps overstated, but until very recently—fifteen or twenty years or so—our organizational systems were just that. They were designed to display in graphic form—organization charts, flowcharts, timetables, and immutable plans—how we were to operate our organizations and manage our people. Just follow those master plans and rules and—presto—our organizations would run. Geniuses dreamed up these systems with the assumption that any average person would be able to plug in and do a reasonably good job without risking a collapse of the organization.

And it made our jobs easier. But something happened. One, we discovered that it wasn't really working. Two, if it had ever worked, then our organizations outgrew it and, to top it off, the world of work changed so radically that the old rules could no longer apply.

In the midst of these changes came a flurry of responses—everything from Total Quality Management (TQM) to Reengineering to the Learning Organization. Changes did take place, yet in the workplace there still seems to be overwork, frustration, discontent, and, in many places, a general malaise bordering on serious morale problems.

Yet unemployment is low, and people are generally better off economically than they were before.

So what's missing? I submit that what has been missing is a deeper connection with our work, a connection that transcends position and power and money, a connection that earlier generations had but that we seem not to have.

I call that connection, that deeper meaning, the spirit of work. Before getting into the meat of this book—the ideas and techniques for applying your spirit every day—let's talk a bit about that subject people have trouble talking about. Let's try to put into words something that almost cannot be put into words. Perhaps the best way to begin is with a poem.

RECESSIONS
Why do we keep on keeping on,
in the midst of such pressure,
when business is no good for no reason,
when everything done right turns out wrong,
when the Fed does something
and interest rates do something
and somebody's notion of consumer confidence does something
and the dogs won't eat the dog food?
What keeps us working late at night
and going back every morning,
living on coffee and waiting for things to bottom out,
crunching numbers as if some answer
lay buried in a computer
and not out among the people who
suddenly and for no reason
are leaving their money in their pockets
and the products on the shelves?
Why don't we just say to hell with it
instead of trying again,
instead of meandering into somebody's office
with half an idea,
hoping she'll have the other half,
hoping what sometimes happens will happen,
that thing, that click, that moment
when two or three of us
gathered together or hanging out
get hit by something we've never tried

but know we can make work the first time?
Could that be it,
that we do all the dull stuff
just for those times
when a revelation rises among us
like something borning,
a new life, another hope,
like something not visible catching the sun,
like a prayer answered?

I wish I could tell you that the way we humans most often connect with one another is through joy and celebration. Those things are important connectors, to be sure, but it is through our loss, our sadness, and our disappointments that we most often feel the deepest connections. Think about it for a minute.

Have you ever had a serious illness or a death in your family? When that happened, how did your coworkers respond? Were they there for you? Did they send you expressions of comfort, of sympathy, of support? Did they try to make things easier for you on the job during those days?

I know that for most people, the answers to the last three questions are yes, yes, and yes.

Here's another question: Were you surprised in those sad circumstances to find that one of those supportive and comforting coworkers turned out to be someone you'd always had negative feelings about? Perhaps you had thought that coworker was overbearing or officious or disruptive or obstructive. If so, I'm not surprised.

When that happened, you discovered a very important truth, one that should underlie our attitudes when we are with other people: All of us—whoever we are, whatever jobs we hold, and however we look—are more similar than dissimilar. Underneath it all, we have very similar hopes and fears, desires and ambitions. We love, we celebrate, we suffer loss, and we grieve.

This simple fact transcends everything else about us, and this simple fact is the foundation of an attitude that can truly transform the workplace if only we will learn and practice a few guidelines for how to be and how to behave.

There's a line from an old spiritual that goes "Everybody talkin' about heaven ain't goin' there." I've thought of that line many times over the years. I thought about it when I heard some executives talk about TQM, then watched them try to use it to put the squeeze on employees. I thought about it when I heard much hoopla about "teams" while watching many companies use teams as a dodge for downsizing. I thought about it when I heard managers talk grandly about empowerment while still looking over the shoulders of, and micromanaging, their employees. As the spiritual says, it's a lot easier to talk about something than to put it into practice.

No news about that. But now there's another subject, one that is getting a lot of attention lately because it has the potential to bring about enormous changes in the workplace, in the lives of employees generally, and in your own life specifically.

The subject is spirituality and work.

Now I can hear the groans and sighs of those who must be thinking, "Here's another one of those touchy-feely 'Let's all love one another so we can be productive' books by a self-appointed guru."

If you're thinking that, you have every right to. And my purpose is not to try to talk you out of that skepticism, but to talk about how you have to be, not what you have to do, to put the spirit of work to work, to become a leader who serves rather than one who expects to be served.

I say "the spirit of work" to distinguish your spirituality at work from the more personal spirituality that comes from your relationship with the sacred, with God, with a higher power. Certainly the spirituality you bring to work is derived from the same source—but the expression of it is in another context, which is, "How does your spirituality find expression in the workplace, in your attitude about your work, in your relationships with your employees, peers, colleagues, customers, vendors, and others?" That's the question and the challenge, because it is in your attitude and behavior as well as in your relationships that your spirituality expresses itself at work—an expression that is most often manifest as service.

I've said it before, I say it again: Business is about people. Business is of, by, about, and for people. And it is ultimately how you are with those people that makes all the difference in whether or not your spirituality finds an expression within the context of your work.

This is not about some arbitrary decision. "Okay, now, let's all be spiritual, then we can be happier and more productive that way." This is not a trick or a gimmick. This isn't a technique. It's not even a process. It is a conscious choice about how you choose to be and about how you choose to live your life at home as well as at work.

I know there's always the risk of sounding too otherworldly, too disconnected from the reality of the workplace, when I talk about being versus doing, so let me state clearly my belief that what you do at work is a direct reflection of how you are. If you want to make that connection between your spirituality and your work, then the proof of it, in other people's eyes, is in what you do and the way you choose to do whatever it is, from an appraisal to running a meeting to, yes, even firing someone.

I want to offer five ways of being that will move you toward an unswerving attitude of service, thus toward the most meaningful expression of your spirituality at work. If you can embrace these five attributes, then you can make the best use of all the ideas and techniques offered in this book.

FIVE WAYS OF BEING

Be Authentic

Be Vulnerable

Be Accepting

Be Present

Be Useful

The five ways of being are: be authentic, be vulnerable, be accepting, be present, and be useful.

Be Authentic

What does being authentic mean? Simply stated, it means be who you are. Be the same person in every circumstance. Hold to the same values in whatever role you have. Always be your real self. Maybe the best way to say this is to ask if you've heard the expression "He's real." That's what I'm taking about. Being real.

I recall once in my career when I was in serious conflict with the vice president who was over my department. I had been given his job and felt, probably a little arrogantly, that it was mine to do and define. We were in conflict from the beginning. Finally, I got a very attractive offer to go to New York in a substantial position in our industry. So I resigned.

My big boss, the CEO of the company, asked by phone that I hold my letter of resignation until he could fly back from New York and meet with me. I agreed but offered no promises. My new employer was waiting for the go-ahead to prepare a press release. This was no maneuver on my part. I don't believe in ultimatums or maneuvers of that type; in fact, it would not have been authentic for me to try to pull such a maneuver.

At four in the afternoon, I went into the CEO's office and handed him the letter. He read it. He looked at me, right in the eye, put his hand on my arm, and said, "I've been such a jerk, and I'm sorry. I knew this was a big problem, but I hoped it would go away. I should have known better. I should have known that the structure I set up did not free you to do the creative job I expected. I'm sorry. I'll change it. I need you here to help carry out the vision. Please stay."

To make the story short, I stayed. I didn't stay for more money or power or position. I stayed because I believed the CEO. I had always believed in him as a visionary leader, but it was at that moment that I got the measure of him as an honest, authentic human being—one willing to admit his mistakes, who did not allow his sense of his position, his ego, to prevent him from apologizing to someone lower in the hierarchy.

This may seem simple enough on the surface, but the fact is that much of our conditioning is against being authentic. In the process of socializing us, of teaching us how to be in the world, our parents taught us to not say some of what we were feeling or thinking. This carries over to the workplace, where we are taught, through direct instruction or through our own observation, that some subjects are "taboo around here." We learn the politics of when to speak and when not to speak, of what to say, of how to handle bad news. We learn to fudge the budget or cover our rears with memos.

I'm not talking about dishonesty, though that could be considered radical inauthenticity. I'm talking about how we are conditioned to not be true to ourselves.

I recently worked with a top manager who had two major management flaws, both having to do with his unwillingness to be authentic. He believes that telling people what they want to hear is the most effective way to manage them, whether or not he really believes what he's telling them. He is always sure to use language that is slippery, that gives him an out if he doesn't want to do what he has led them to expect he will do. For instance, when asked about a policy that I knew he instituted and fully supported, he replied, "Good point. I could be persuaded to take another look at that one."

Notice that he didn't say, "I will take another look," or, "You've persuaded me to take another look," though that is what the employee was led to believe. When I, as a consultant, called the manager on his language, he even tried to pull it on me.

"I didn't lie," he said. "I really could be persuaded to take another look." Slippery, slippery—and not the language of authenticity. Authenticity means much more than being technically truthful.

Another senior manager I know is fond of committees or, as he calls them, "work groups." But here's the way it works. The group spends time studying a situation of the manager's choosing, then works out recommendations and sends the manager a report. He then red-pencils the report and sends it back. Then it comes back. Then he red-pencils it again with suggestions. Finally, when the committee recommends what he wanted done in the first place, he approves the report.

When I asked him why he didn't just tell them how he wanted it done, rather than putting them through all the work and frustration, he replied, "I saw it as a learning experience for them."

That is not an authentic way to provide a learning experience.

Learning experiences are important, and it is important to mentor people and help them learn. But realize that mentoring is also about helping people learn to be themselves. You do that by honoring what is good and unique about those you are mentoring, not by trying to bend them to your image. That's playing God.

Being authentic is, first, knowing yourself, then being yourself. Authenticity derives from our deepest, truest selves. How do we come to know ourselves? Only through what can be called spiritual disciplines: silence, meditation, prayer. And certainly, sometimes, traditional therapy or groups dedicated to self-exploration.

If you are truly authentic then you'll also . . .

Be Vulnerable

Back in the 1980s, during the farm crisis, one of my company's magazines, *Successful Farming*, decided to sponsor a major conference on alternative agriculture. We decided to give farmers all over the country a chance to come to our headquarter's city and participate. The conference would be free to the farmers, and we promised to get them good prices on room and board. We would even charter buses at no cost to transport the farmers. As you might imagine, this was an expensive proposition with no apparent payoff, but that's the kind of relationship we felt we had with our readers, our customers, who were suffering.

The letters began to pour in. Many of them came to the CEO.

At an annual employees' meeting in New York, at the big luncheon, the CEO referred to what we were doing and to some of the letters he received. He began to read one: "We're dying out here," it said, "and you're the only ones who seem to care." The CEO could hardly finish the sentence because he became so choked up. He himself had grown up in a rural area and could feel deeply the words he was reading.

You might imagine that crowd of New Yorkers was cynical or hard-edged in its response. Not at all. Here was our big boss who, in sharing the letters as part of his business presentation, let us all see and experience his own sympathy and grief about what those letters represented, as well as his pride about what we were doing. He did not intend to choke up; it was certainly not a technique, a cynical ploy.

The paradox in being vulnerable is that it also requires you to be courageous. What does *vulnerable* mean? Wearing your feelings on your sleeve? Sharing your pain? Tearing up at a moment's notice? No. Doing any of those things as some kind of "technique" would be neither authentic nor truly vulnerable.

Basically, being vulnerable means being honest with your feelings in the context of your work; being open with your doubts and fears and concerns about an idea, an employee's performance, or your own performance; and being able to admit mistakes openly, particularly with your employees. Simply saying, "I was wrong," and meaning it, embracing it, is an expression of vulnerability and, I believe, is a sign of being spiritually attuned and aware.

Being vulnerable takes a great deal of courage because it means letting go of the old notions of control, forgetting forever the illusion that you can be in control. Too many of us think that our power comes from our ability to maintain control. To the contrary, our power comes from realizing that we can't be in control and that we must depend on others.

Despite the image of the rugged individual, you really don't succeed at anything in an organization by yourself. It's a myth we need to be rid of.

But just as we are conditioned against being authentic, we are conditioned against being vulnerable. Men, especially, are taught to be tough, to not show their feelings. This is an old story, and too much has been made of the gender differences in this regard, but we should recognize that all of us have been taught to cover up our emotions. But there simply is no way to be authentic without revealing our true selves, and that means revealing our emotions, how we feel about the work, the workplace, and one another.

I include anger in this definition. Is there a spiritual way to show anger? Yes.

Expressing anger honestly is very different from acting in anger. You can properly express anger, but you can't act properly if you act in anger. One can be called spiritually appropriate; the other is the opposite.

Vulnerability has an aspect of empathy as well, the ability to put yourself in the other's shoes, to view the world or the situation from the other's viewpoint. So . . .

Be Accepting

Acceptance is more important than approval. I believe this is true in friendship and marriage and parenting, as well as in professional relationships. I have observed that most of the conflicts in a workplace are more concerned with style and personality than with product or process. Thus, communities of work, from teams to large departments, will become dysfunctional unless the art of acceptance becomes the norm.

A lot of organizations are emphasizing teams for more productivity and a generally better working environment. But the fact is that teams often don't work because the expectation is that everything will be hunky-dory all the time, that real team members will always agree. I'm sure you've heard it said of someone who disagrees with other members of the team that he or she is "not a team player."

The art of acceptance does not imply that you accept everyone's ideas without critical analysis, discussion, and judgment—only that you accept the ideas as valid for discussion and review, and that you focus on the ideas themselves, not on the person who presented them.

It also means that you accept and embrace disagreement as a human part of the process of work.

If you are to express your spirituality fully, if you are to achieve the goal of servant leadership, then you must abandon any dualistic notion of winners and losers. My goodness, we have done way too much to turn the workplace and business into some kind of war, or at least high-contact sport. But the truth is that we are participants together. All can win; nobody has to lose. Authentic people never feel themselves to be losers; thus, they can never be losers. Others may call you a loser, but that's only because they have some need to feel that they are winners—something they simply can't do unless they can think of someone else as a loser.

Authentic people do not get into this trap. Authentic people accept others without judgment, just as they want to be accepted, without the need for approval or disapproval.

Being accepting is possible only if you can . . .

Be Present

When I say "be present," you might be tempted to look around and say, "I'm here, ain't I?" I can't argue with that, but being present is not just being here or there, but having your whole self available at all times—available to yourself as you try to bring all your values to bear on the work at hand, and available to others as you respond to the problems and issues and challenges of team members, colleagues, managers, employees, vendors, and customers.

This is a difficult task because of the pressures of the past and the future. We're always trying to learn from the past, and if we're fulfilling our full management role, we're always planning for the future. So being attuned to all your management responsibilities while living in the present and focusing on the here and now sometimes seems impossible. It often seems counterintuitive as well.

But believe me, the effect on those around you is palpable. When they see you remaining centered and grounded in the midst of whatever perceived crisis is at hand—and there is usually one crisis on a regular basis in most workplaces—they will be more assured and confident in their own actions.

Conversely, when they see you agitated, worried, stressed, short-tempered, and distracted, then they become the same way, only worse because they're worried that you might take it (whatever *it* is) out on them.

So be present. Think about it. Concentrate on it. Do you want a little, almost trivial-sounding, ten-second tool for quickly helping you come back to center? Try this meditative technique I learned a long time ago and still use to this day. In fact, I used it before I began writing today.

Think about something that makes you smile: a loved one, a child, an experience you had, a great vacation. Just visualize what makes you smile.

Now close your eyes, take as deep a breath as you can, hold it for a couple of seconds, think about what makes you smile, then smile, and exhale slowly. Open your eyes. Try this a couple of times a day, perhaps once in the morning and once in the afternoon. It's a ten-second investment in being present. Guaranteed.

Now, if you are authentic, vulnerable, accepting, and present, there's only one other aspect to manifesting your spirituality at work. And that is simply to . . .

Be Useful

I have to smile a little as I write this, because I recall my grandmother saying to me—it seemed several times a day—"Jimmy, make yourself useful around here."

And that goes to the very heart of this book: service. The most important thing you can be as a leader is useful. Let me put that another way. The late Robert Greenleaf wrote and lectured extensively on the servant leader. He also established the highly regarded Greenleaf Center for Servant Leadership in Indianapolis. Underlying Dr. Greenleaf's work and my own urging to make yourself useful is the fundamental concept of being of service to others.

Another way to think of this is as a resource for your people. One of the primary functions of the manager/leader is to assure that people get the resources they need to do the job. To be a leader who serves, you must think of yourself as—and indeed must be—their principal resource.

Clearly this requires a change of orientation for many people. After all, you worked hard to get to be a manager, to get to be the boss. And now I'm telling you to be a resource.

Yes.

Because this concept of serving others is an essential part of what I believe about leadership, let me offer you a list of six things I believe about leadership:

1. Leadership is not about controlling people; it's about caring for people and being a useful resource for people.

2. Leadership is not about being boss; it's about being present for people and building a community at work.

3. Leadership is not about holding on to territory; it's about letting go of ego, bringing your spirit to work, being your best and most authentic self.

4. Leadership is less concerned with pep talks and more concerned with creating a place in which people can do good work, can find meaning in their work, and can bring their spirits to work.

5. Leadership, like life, is largely a matter of paying attention.

6. Leadership requires love.

I'm sure that what I've written here so far could be considered almost antithetical to what you've been taught to believe about management and leadership. But that's because so much of what we think we know about leadership is based on old concepts of power. In organizations we spend a lot of time figuring out who has power and how much we have. It's only natural that if we think we have power, some of us seem to have to prove it by flexing our management muscles.

But true power comes from the people. It comes from gaining the trust and support of the people who then give you the power. Power is like love. The more you try to give it to others, the more it just seems to flow to you naturally.

If you, in a leadership position, can attain the authenticity, vulnerability, acceptance, presence, and usefulness to become a servant leader, then I believe that is the highest manifestation of your spirituality in the context of work.

CHAPTER TWO

Understanding the Three Aspects of Vision

THE PROBLEM WITH WORDS like *mission* and *vision* is that they are given to so many different interpretations they begin to lose their meaning. More important, they begin to lose their value to an organization and its people.

In fact, ever since former President George Bush referred to "the vision thing," many people, particularly in the media, often ridicule the whole idea of "vision" as if it was just another semantic trick, another piece of political rhetoric or, in the case of business, of "management-speak."

Furthermore, the top management of many companies developed mission statements or vision statements (or both) in all the wrong ways. Rather than involve employees in the process of defining the vision, top management took it upon themselves to develop a statement which then, in top-down mode, was given to the employees and the public.

I fantasize it happening something like this. At a management team meeting of, say, Ajax Apparatus, Inc., someone says, "You know, those guys over at Acme Apparatus have a mission statement, and we don't have one."

"You mean a vision statement, don't you?" another member of the team responds.

"Mission, vision, whatever. They have one and we don't."

The realization that a competitor has something that Ajax doesn't galvanizes the team and they decide, "We need a mission or vision statement, too."

"How are we going to get one?" asks the CEO. "Any ideas?"

"I know," says the vice president for communications. "Our agency does great vision statements. Let's get them to do one."

So they do. They agency produces a statement, the management team approves it, and it is then printed in the company newsletter, made into posters, mailed to financial analysts and stockholders, and finally made into a beautiful quilt or rendered on parchment with stunning calligraphy to hang on the CEO's wall. And then what?

Everybody forgets about it.

Why? Chances are the employees forget about it because it is so removed from their everyday work lives and from their understanding of their jobs that they consider it irrelevant.

And they're right. Chances are it is irrelevant. Unfortunately, "irrelevant" describes far too many vision or mission statements that are promulgated by organizations these days.

The problem, I think, is not with the intention to do something good. It is with a misunderstanding about the nature of these statements and what they are supposed to mean for the overall organization and for its people.

In my work with companies, I have found it helpful to offer a definition and an explanation of vision that I believe works in several ways. One, it works to inspire people about the company and their own involvement in the company. Two, it works to define specifically what the company does and why. Three, it works to define interpersonal relationships or social architecture (call it "culture" if you wish) within the company.

And another thing: This approach provides an understanding of "vision" that is most consonant with the kind of workplace the servant leader aspires to create.

An organization's "vision" should be conceived as the confluence of three interrelated but distinct aspects: purpose, mission, and values.

An organization's "vision" should be conceived as the confluence of three interrelated but distinct aspects:

purpose, mission, and values. An understanding of vision must include all three, and any articulation of vision should include all three.

To explain briefly: purpose describes the greater reason for a company's or organization's being in the world; mission describes what the company or organization does to fulfill its purpose; values describe how the people are together as they go about performing their mission in order to fulfill their purpose.

Purpose

The definition of purpose begins with the question, "Why are we here?" We recognize this question as the source of much philosophical and religious inquiry into the nature of human existence. We recognize the question as the first step in the search for meaning. Some say the question is not answerable; others say the answer depends on each individual; yet others say the answer is spelled out in one religious text or another.

The question is as vital to the life of an organization as it is to the life of a person, but in the case of an organization, the question is and must be answerable. Without an understanding of purpose, an organization will become dysfunctional (and many have). It is an understanding and a sense of purpose that provides the beacon that illuminates the potential for finding meaning in every single job, whether CEO or mail room clerk.

In business workshops, as you might guess, the quickest answer I receive to the question, "Why are we here?" is, "To make a profit." But that's the wrong answer. A company's purpose is not to make a profit. Making a profit is important to be sure, and we'll get to that a little later, but making a profit is not the purpose. It is only one of the means of fulfilling the purpose.

The purpose itself must be understood as an over-arching reason for being. Let me use two examples from my own experience. For several years in my career, I was editor in chief of *Better Homes and Gardens* magazine (among many others). If I asked you to speculate on the purpose of *Better Homes and Gardens*, you might say, "Show pretty pictures and recipes for people to look at and perhaps copy." Wrong. A more careful reader might say, "To present articles and ideas for people to use in their homes and family life." That would be closer but still wrong.

The purpose of *Better Homes and Gardens* magazine, as we articulated it in those days, was to provide people with ideas, information, and inspiration to help enhance and enrich their family lives, including their relationships as well as their physical environment.

In recent years, I've served on the board of a prominent media company in the natural products field, thus have worked with several natural products companies and their management. Most of these companies describe their purpose as "to make a better world by helping people and their families lead healthier lives." Each company may use different words, but essentially this is the purpose.

I know a public relations firm that describes its purpose as "helping people have a voice that will be heard. . . ."

The "purpose" aspect of vision should always address the "Why are we here?" question in what might be called high-minded ways. And the answer should always contain language that helps everyone involved with the organization understand and focus on why they themselves are there. To put that another way, the purpose of an organization helps people define the purpose of their own involvement and helps them align their own purpose with the organization's purpose.

For instance, if an editor or a writer feels that his or her purpose has to do with serving people who are interested in spectator sports or popular culture, then chances are, Better Homes and Gardens is not the right place for that person to be working.

The purpose of an organization might evolve over the years, but if it changes quickly or radically, something's wrong.

Mission

The mission question is simply, "What do we do?" By extension, it's, "What do we do in order to fulfill our purpose?"

For a business, this is where the "make a profit" answer begins to fit, but of course it's more complicated than that, because making a profit requires that the company and its employees produce something, a product or service, that fulfills the purpose with enough perceived value that people—customers—are willing to pay for that product or service. Simple enough to say, but sometimes not so simple to understand or to execute.

More than one company has lost sight of its mission, sometimes in the name of "diversification" or "product extension" or simply "growth." You may recall the turmoil of the eighties as companies "reengineered" and "downsized," selling businesses and shutting down others. Often the explanation given was that the company had "lost focus" and now needed to get back to its "core competencies" and "stick to its knitting." All ways of saying that the companies had lost sight of their mission.

In the seventies, it seemed a good idea to some that Better Homes and Gardens should go into the residential real estate franchise business, in effect licensing the name Better Homes and Gardens to real estate agents around the country. The linkage here is obvious. The name would provide a kind of quality endorsement to the homes themselves.

The corporation of which *Better Homes and Gardens* was the leading product, however, was (and is) a media company, not a real estate company. Its purpose was information; its mission was media. Several of us in the magazine group did not support this extension of the name, not because we thought there was anything wrong or unworthy about the business itself but because in our opinion, it was far outside the mission.

Our mission was to create magazines that fulfilled the purpose by providing, in a certain printed format, the ideas, information, and inspiration to help people enhance and enrich their home and family lives. It was not to sell houses.

The company has now sold the real estate franchise business, and has licensed the name to another company. Enough said about that.

Part of the mission for businesses may also be expressed in financial terms: profit, return on equity, return on investment, enhanced stockholder value, and so on. Still, these financial results are not the mission itself; they are part of the measurement of the success, or lack of it, of the "doing" part of the mission.

Can a business accomplish the mission and fulfill the purpose without making a profit? Yes, but probably not for long because financial results are an integral part of a business's mission. Certainly a start-up business should accomplish the "doing" part of its mission and fulfill its purpose while losing money in the investment phase, or it'll never get past that phase.

But it's also true that if a company focuses only on the "bottom line," that means the organization is obsessed with only the mission aspect of its vision, or it doesn't have a true vision at all.

It is important to understand that your mission can change for any number of reasons, but your purpose rarely, if ever, changes. There may come the day when magazines are obsolete as printed material, so a media company's mission may shift from making magazines on paper to providing information online, or both, as some companies now do. But the purpose will not have changed.

Mission also has to do with goals, organizational and individual. We'll talk about goal setting and performance standards in chapter 5, but realize here that accomplishing goals is not the same as fulfilling either the organization's or your personal purpose.

Values

A discussion of values begins with the question, "How are we together as we go about performing our mission in order to fulfill our purpose?" Now we come to the basic material with which the servant leader works in shaping an organization or, as I will often refer to it, a "community of work." The values within an organization derive from the people, to be sure, but it is a primary and essential responsibility of the servant leader to help guide the development of these values into a long-term framework of behavior that will benefit the organization and everyone in it.

Values are fundamentally about interpersonal relationships or social architecture or culture. I think of values in an organization as having two closely interrelated aspects: organizational values and personal values.

In conducting values workshops, I ask participants to finish the following sentences: "We want to work in an organization that values _____." And "We want to work with people who value _____."

This exercise allows the participants to define their own Utopian situation, a workplace and colleagues of their own creation.

Then I ask them to finish these sentences: "This organization values _____." And "These people value _____." This exercise allows the participants to realistically face their own situation.

The result is usually a gap between how they'd like things to be and how things are. No surprise about that. The important insight people learn from this "values gap analysis" is that everyone has a role, indeed a responsibility, to participate in determining the values that they, together, want to manifest toward one another and toward their work as they go about accomplishing their mission in order to fulfill their purpose.

In turn, management people learn what the expectations are regarding the values the employees want the company (management) to manifest as part of the working environment.

If, for instance, one of the personal values is honesty, this means that management must exhibit honesty. One thing leads to another. Creating an honest environment means a workplace of open and honest communication, no secrets, no favored groups who are "in the know" to the exclusion of others, sharing of plans and results, and a commitment to timely appraisals, critiques, and feedback.

If one of the personal values is trust, this means the leaders must trust the people and, in turn, must be trustworthy. Again, one thing leads to another. Creating a trusting environment means a workplace in which people are part of the decisions about the goals to be accomplished, then are trusted to do their work without constant supervision (looking over their shoulders), in which rewards and recognition are based on results and not on favoritism, in which rules and policies are as few as possible and as flexible as possible in accommodating individual human needs. And so on.

Here are some other values that emerged from a recent exercise like the ones just described: integrity, respect, teamwork, individuality, hard work, balance between work and home, compassion, optimism, courage, diversity, sensitivity, passion, kindness, loyalty, forgiveness, humor, patience, risk taking, change.

The purpose of these exercises is basically to guide people into focusing on what their values are and how they would like them to be. Without a sense of how we want to be together in this enterprise, in this mutual endeavor, in this community of work, we will have no framework for how we will behave toward one another. Without a framework, the culture will sort of evolve on its own and, predictably, will become dysfunctional from time to time, if not all the time.

What does this mean? How does this look in real life?

Without a framework of understood and shared values like those just listed, a company frequently will become a collection of individual fiefdoms (departments) in which management people are aggressive and competitive with one another, jealous of their prerogatives, paranoid about their positions, and generally distrustful of their employees. They operate with the attitude that, left to their own devices, the employees will always do the wrong thing.

Accordingly, the employees behave the same way, forming cliques not only of their own departments but also within their own departments. People are "in" or "out," few people trust others outside their own clique, and no one trusts management.

I suspect this sounds familiar. It is not unlike many top-down, command-control organizations, and not just the ones of yesteryear either. They exist today even in Silicon Valley.

I do not mean to suggest that some of the organizations that operate in this mode are not successful in financial terms. To the contrary, this kind of organization, believe it or not, often operates very efficiently, particularly when business is good and financial rewards are available to partially offset the discontents of the people.

But efficiency is not the same as effectiveness, and it is the latter to which servant leadership most concerns itself. If the people are led in a way that allows them all to be effective in their work, then efficiency follows. It does not work the other way around.

The servant leader knows that people who work within a framework of good values and who behave toward one another in accordance with those values can create a community of work that will be effective over the long term, that will be productive and appropriately efficient, and thus will accomplish the mission that fulfills their purpose.

A leader with this tripartite understanding of vision must also realize that this same definition applies to personal as well as organizational vision. Ideally, servant leaders will have shaped their own vision according to three questions: What is my purpose in being here, in this world, in this life, in this profession, in this job? What must I do to accomplish my current mission in order to fulfill my purpose? How am I to be, how am I to behave, how am I to manifest my values toward others within my own life as I go about accomplishing my mission in order to fulfill my purpose?

Once you, the leader, have inculcated this concept of vision into your own consciousness, the next step is to help others in your care—your colleagues and employees—develop their own vision.

The confluence and alignment of these personal visions with the organization's vision will then become the most powerful possible determinant of success.

PART TWO

Servant Leader as Manager: The Everyday Nuts and Bolts

NOT EVERY MANAGER CAN become a leader, but every leader must possess and demonstrate good management knowledge and skills.

Some people aspiring to leadership don't want to hear this; their perception is that leaders have only to be concerned about the "big picture." In defense of that perception, they like to quote the famous definition, "Managers concentrate on doing things right, and leaders concentrate on doing the right thing."

I quote that definition myself, but it is not about an abdication of good management skills, and it's certainly not about an ignorance of those skills. Instead, it is meant to define what a manager must move beyond (focusing on how to do) in order to become a leader (focusing on what to do and how to be). Consider the famous painting of George Washington crossing the Delaware. The folks who think that leadership does not require good management skills probably think that because Washington is pictured as standing in the boat, his gaze fixed on the far shore, he never had to learn to row the boat or that he could not directly supervise the rowing. This may seem a silly example, but in its simplicity it illustrates three functions within an organization: workers (they're the ones rowing), supervisors or managers (they're overseeing the rowing, assuring that each person knows the job and has the equipment to do it, and that the workload is equitably distributed), and leaders (Washington knows where they're going and why, and we presume he has to the best of his ability articulated a vision of victory).

While the psychological, emotional, and spiritual preparation for leadership begins on the inside, as part of the inner life, the organizational preparation for leadership begins with the fundamentals of management.

The difference in preparing for servant leadership is that the fundamentals of management must be practiced with the same attitude of service. It is impossible to be a top-down, command-control, top-sergeant manager and expect to evolve somehow into a servant leader.

The servant leader/manager is faced with all the challenges of any other manager: finding good people, training them, helping them understand a workplace in which servant leadership is dominant, using the organizational tools such as job descriptions and performance standards to achieve clarity about what is to be done, and providing the resources to make people productive.

In this section, I will concentrate on these tools of management, and in the next chapters will provide guidance in facing some of today's realities of management and leadership.

CHAPTER THREE

Finding the Right People

BY THE "RIGHT PEOPLE" I mean people who will accept, and flourish in, the servant leadership culture—particularly managers who demonstrate the capacity to become such leaders themselves. How can you be sure that the managers you hire will embody and promulgate the concepts of servant leadership?

Nothing takes the place of your own impressions gained during a personal interview, of course, but I have developed a simple questionnaire that can provide insights into the precepts that a potential manager holds about management itself. You may want to have the job candidate take time to think about the questions and provide written answers to discuss during the interview. Or you may want to simply use this questionnaire as a guide in interviewing. You will probably want to add questions and perhaps even put these questions into your own words. Clearly this questionnaire is not about specific skills and is not meant to be. I have assumed that you will already have determined appropriate skills, experience, and professional qualifications.

QUESTIONNAIRE

1. What is your own personal purpose in pursuing the professional life you've chosen?

2. Do you think that most people want to do a good job?

   If the answer is no, end the interview as soon as possible.

3. If the answer is yes, then ask, "Do you think, then, that most people will make every effort to do a good job if trusted to do a good job?"

   If the answer is no, end the interview as soon as possible.

Note: One of the basic foundations of servant leadership is trust. Far too many managers try to operate without trust between managers and employees as a basic value. I suggest that a manager who does not believe that most people will do a good job if trusted to do a good job is not a candidate for servant leadership.

4. Would you rather be thought of as a manager or as a team member?

The obvious answer to this is, "Team member," so you must follow up with the question, "Why?"

The answer you're looking for must have something to do with the importance of being thought of not as boss but as colleague. At the same time, you want to hear that the manager can never abdicate accountability for results even while not functioning as a traditional "boss." This is tricky because your candidate must understand the need to be among the people, providing resources and serving, while at the same time never losing sight of the fact that he or she is responsible for the well-being of those people and is accountable for their performance as well as for the results they achieve.

5. What is your attitude and philosophy regarding your responsibility for your employees'

whole life, not just professional life? In other words, should you have a concern for an employee's health and well-being outside the workplace? What about a concern for the health and well-being of an employee's family?

These are discussion questions with no absolute right answers, but you want these answers to be a balance between an appropriate concern for achieving the results of the organization while considering the individual human needs of employees. A person hoping to become a servant leader must recognize that effectiveness and productivity are directly affected by situations and occurrences outside the workplace. At this point, you want the candidate to at least demonstrate a recognition of this. You should not expect details of how he or she might respond to specific situations, but this is a fertile subject for exploring a person's basic management philosophy.

6. What are the qualities or characteristics you admire most, or that you think are most important, in a leader/manager?

You may have your own expectations about this answer, but those characteristics should include some of these: fairness, honesty, trust, sensitivity, respect, integrity, openness, and authenticity.

7. A business leader's primary responsibility is to:
   a. stockholders (owners).
   b. customers.
   c. vendors.
   d. employees.
   e. community at large.
   f. all of the above equally.

   The answer is f.

8. Which of these, in your opinion, are the most important characteristics of a workplace? Pick three.
   a. Everyone likes one another.
   b. There is no disagreement.
   c. There is an attitude of open and honest communication.
   d. People are free to express criticism—of one another, of you, of policies, of the company—without retribution or punishment.

e. All disagreements are worked out before being brought to your attention.

f. There's a consistent effort by management to hear every opinion before a decision is made.

g. The majority rules.

h. People generally depend on you—management—for decisions.

i. Company policies and procedures are judged to be in the best interest of all and are never questioned.

j. Communication flows according to hierarchy and chain of command.

k. The best ideas prevail; hierarchy is not a factor.

You want to see three of these: c, d, f, and k.

9. A company leader's primary concern must be:

a. profit (earnings).

b. customer service.

c. employee needs.

d. survival.

e. product quality.

f. all of the above equally.

All of these are important, and this question can lead to a follow-up discussion. Most experts would agree that survival is primary. In other words, you would never sacrifice the whole enterprise for any of the others. The caveat, however, is that you also would never violate the law or engage in unethical conduct just to save the company. After survival, the servant leader will put employee needs, if not above, then at least equal with the others.

10. If you could create the perfect, Utopian workplace, how would it look? How would people relate to one another, how would people be recognized and rewarded, how would power be expressed?

11. If you could write your own epitaph, something to appear on your tombstone, what would it say about you as a person and as a manager?

CHAPTER FOUR

Training the Servant Leader

SERVANT LEADERSHIP DOES NOT come naturally or easily to people whose experience has been limited to organizations in which the command-control, hierarchal management style is the norm. Unfortunately this style still includes the majority of organizations in the world. Yet I have found that even in the most apparently top-down organizations, there are pockets of the new leadership, so your potential leaders may come to you with some experience beyond the norm. But don't count on it.

The questionnaire in chapter 3 will give you insights about the people you hire, but what about those you inherit if you're the new boss on the scene? And what if you yourself are a recent convert to servant leadership? Perhaps this happened because you decided that the old ways were not working as well or you didn't feel fulfilled as the kind of leader you were and wanted to embrace servant leadership. How will your employees respond to this rather dramatic change, and what can you do to help them transition to a new kind of workplace?

First understand and accept these realities: (1) The transition to a culture of servant leadership cannot be made overnight. If you change yourself, you've already changed the workplace environment, so be happy with that for a while as you become more proficient at manifesting the attributes of servant leadership and modeling those for others. But know also that changing yourself is only the first step. (2) Some people will be slower than others to adapt to the culture. (3) Some people, employees as well as managers, will actively resist the change. (4) Some will never adapt.

> *The transition to a culture of servant leadership cannot be made overnight.*

It is probably normal to expect that the way you choose to serve and lead will be welcomed with open arms by all. After all, aren't the people going to benefit directly? Aren't their lives going to be easier, freer, and more fulfilled than they were under the old, repressive way of doing things?

While the answers to these questions are yes, that doesn't mean people will automatically trust or accept the new way.

I received a call from a manager who had attended one of my workshops and whom I had counseled about his own growth as a leader and his intentions to be a more spiritual, empowering leader. Unfortunately, he had not sought counsel as to how he should proceed in introducing the culture of servant leadership to his department. He was almost distraught on the phone.

"It's not working," he said.

"What do you mean?" I asked.

"I mean that my people don't like it. They don't like the way I am, and they're not responding."

"Tell me the whole story. Start at the point you first introduced the subject in your workplace."

"Okay," he said. "Here's what I did. I called an all-staff meeting. I wanted to make it a celebration, so I arranged for refreshments and a relaxing setting."

"That's a good start."

"And then I just told them what I had learned from you and others, including some books I'd read, and told them I'd decided to try to create a work environment in which I would still be their boss but would be more of a resource to them. I told them they would have far more empowerment to make their own decisions, to write their own job descriptions, and so on. All the stuff you talked about."

"Then what?"

"I asked for questions. That's when I got the shock."

"Don't tell me. They immediately asked a lot of specific questions about specific projects, and who would decide this and who would decide that, and who would have authority for this or that, and so on, right?"

"Right. They seemed preoccupied with who was going to have power to make decisions and who they should go to for those decisions. They didn't seem to get it that they were going to make a lot of the decisions themselves."

I told him that I was not surprised, and that their reaction was the normal reaction to sudden change: fear. And their reaction was normal for anyone suddenly thrust into an unexpected position of responsibility: fear.

"You scared the hell out of them," I said.

"But I was trying to be sensitive and responsive and all those things. I was trying to inspire them about how things were going to be from now on."

"So there's a good lesson for you," I said. "It doesn't matter whether change is positive or negative; if it's sudden, it produces fear or anxiety."

"What should I do now?"

I told him that, fortunately, it was not a desperate situation as he feared; that it would just take some time and some education and training.

I've known managers who, after being inspired to manage in a new way based on concepts of servant leadership and the community of work, including shared decision making, honest and open communication, trust, elimination of destructive competition, and an environment of mutual respect, returned to their workplaces and expected a sudden miracle. They expected that when they took the harnesses off the horses, they'd just run free as the wind, but in fact, they just ran in circles.

Why? The better question is why not? It is completely understandable, and the people are not to be faulted for their reluctance to suddenly embrace the new culture. We have all been deeply conditioned—psychologically, emotionally, culturally, and even spiritually—to accept a certain hierarchy. We learn to worship a powerful parent God who makes rules; if we obey the rules we are to be rewarded, and if we disobey we are to be punished. For the majority of people, this model follows through into their experience with parents, then with teachers.

The structure of most organizations is based on the old Christmas-tree organization chart, first used by the church, then adopted by the military and subsequently by virtually every organization in the Western world up until about the middle of the twentieth century.

In order to bring the concepts of servant leadership to your people, you must prepare them, educate them, train them. I've often heard this comment: "Surely there is some piece of quick and easy advice you give to people who want to engage in the kind of leadership you advocate." In fact, I do have a piece of advice—quick but not so easy—and I offer it to new managers, to would-be servant leaders, and even to parents: When you are tempted to tell someone what to do, instead ask the question, "What do you think you should do now?" Or in an organizational setting, "What do you think we should do?" This is the only quick tip I have, but believe me, it can work magic. Remember, when tempted to tell, ask instead.

The quick tip is just that, only a tip. Beyond that, you should schedule classes or seminars discussing the various styles of leadership and organizational culture. This doesn't have to be heavy stuff, but should enlighten people particularly about the kind of culture you want to create and its advantages over the top-down, hierarchal culture.

You can make reading lists, but that alone won't do it because, sad to say, most people will not read the books. Better to bring in speakers and discussion leaders, show videos, and provide opportunities for response and participation by everyone.

In addition to the formal training, you and your managers must engage people directly in small groups. In fact, you should continue these kinds of gatherings even after you're satisfied that the transition is complete.

When I was president of a major operating group, I had a small session with employees once a week wherever I was, at the corporate headquarters or in a branch office. My assistant would randomly select a group of employees to have coffee with me one morning. The selection was completely without regard for position; a vice president might be sitting next to a mail room clerk. There were nine hundred people in my operating group, so it probably took a year for me to cover everyone. In addition, I suggested that all the department managers have such regular sessions.

The format was simple. People would serve themselves coffee and muffins or doughnuts, then when everyone was settled, we'd go around the table, and people would introduce themselves with a sentence or two describing their jobs and how long they'd been with the company. Then I'd give a general, informal report on the state of the business, how we were doing on our year's goals, including sales, revenue, and so on. I'd talk about any special projects we might have going, new product tests, and results of tests.

After that, I asked for comments on how business looked from their various perspectives and invited questions on any subject. No question was off-limits, and I promised to answer to the best of my ability. If I didn't know the answer, I said so, but promised to get an answer later. After an hour or so, we all returned to our jobs.

As simple and straightforward as they were, these little sessions had an amazing impact. It never failed that I received responses and comments from almost everyone who attended, and their sense of involvement and appreciation was palpable. I believe these coffees did a lot to emphasize the environment of openness and trust we were trying to create.

In the past few years, I have introduced into two separate companies the idea of "the reading of the news." This is a monthly gathering, usually on a Friday afternoon, at which refreshments are served and one person who is chosen ahead of time—sometimes laughingly called the town crier—reads a whole stack of news reports submitted by every department. Then the floor is open for news from anyone. Sometimes it's all company stuff; sometimes it's quite personal—engagements, birthdays, achievements of an employee's children, a

particularly good golf score. Occasionally someone offers a poem or a song. There might be an award or recognition of someone's outstanding performance, either in
the company or in the community.

These meetings offer the double advantage of news
and information along with good fun. In addition, people are given a sense of participation in a community
rather than just doing a job. The mixture of business and
personal news emphasizes that we are all engaged in this
together and that both our professional and personal
lives, while separate, are of interest and concern to one
another. (I should point out the obvious: Some people
are more private than others, and there should never be
any pressure to participate in personal discussions.)

These ideas and techniques are all part of the general
subject of education and training, which must be ongoing. There never comes a time at which anyone can say,
"Well, we've now done the servant leadership thing; time
to move to the next thing." Remember this: The transition to a servant leader workplace is not an episode or an
event; it is a never-ending process of which you are the
most important element. You have to walk the walk and
talk the talk. Your behavior and the example you set are
primary; in addition, you must never let the subject
drop. You have to talk about it and talk about it and talk
about it. There's an old saying in sales: "You gotta tell
them what you're going to tell them, then tell them, then
tell them what you told them."

CHAPTER FIVE

The Tools of the Trade

MY CLIENTS AND WORKSHOP participants are often surprised that I am an avid supporter of such organizational tools as job descriptions, performance standards, performance appraisals, and performance ratings. I also support reward systems directly tied to performance ratings. The surprise comes, I think, because these systems have become identified with the top-down, command-control management style.

Just a couple of years ago, I recommended to a client, a very bright CEO/entrepreneur who had built a large, successful, and growing business, that he needed to inculcate into his company some systems and procedures in order to achieve clarity about what people were to do and how they were to be evaluated.

The CEO had prided himself on building a company that featured an open and honest culture, sensitivity to individual human needs, and mutual respect. In other words, he had worked hard to be a servant leader and had succeeded, but his success brought a larger organization with more people. As the company grew, the daily glitches began to multiply, and there began to be clearly discernible pockets of discontent turning up here and there. People complained that there were too many changes, that they didn't get to finish one project before being pulled off and put on another one. They were often uncertain about what they were to do and about how they were doing.

The company had depended so much on word of mouth and personal contact between top management and the employees that there simply were no adequate systems of job description, performance standards, appraisal, and review.

When I made my proposal, it was the first time my client (and friend) had ever become angry with me. "What is this, Jim?" he shouted. "You know me well enough to know I don't want this kind of corporate crap in my company."

"But Greg, this is a corporation, even though it's your private corporation, and you're getting big enough that you need something like this."

"Why? In two sentences tell me why I need this," he challenged.

"Listen, Greg," I answered, "you know I'm not anything close to what you would call a procedure freak . . ."

"Two sentences," he interrupted.

"I can't do it adequately in two sentences. How about a paragraph?"

He smiled and became a little calmer. "Okay. I know you have my best interests at heart, so give me a paragraph."

"There are several issues," I began, "but the most important one is fairness."

This almost set him off again. "Fairness? Fairness? I pride myself on how fairly we run this company."

"I know you do, and I hope you know that I have enormous admiration for what you've done and how you run this place, but you can't be here all the time. You can't do everything. You have to trust your managers to run with the ball you throw them."

"I do trust them. They know that."

"Yes, but while they reflect your philosophy and style, they really need to be doing things according to the same guidelines and procedures. Otherwise people in different departments who may be doing comparable jobs get treated in different ways."

"Listen to you," he challenged me again. "You're the guy who's always preaching special treatment, responding to people's individual needs, managing people one at a time and not in groups. You taught me that."

"Yes, I did," I said, "but I'm not talking about responding to individual needs, something that should be done personally by individual managers. I'm talking about having minimum standards and procedures by which everyone is assured of fair treatment when it comes to what their jobs are, what is expected, upon what they will be evaluated, and by what guidelines they will be rewarded. Without an agreed-upon system, even the best, most well-meaning managers will be tempted to make arbitrary decisions about these vital matters."

After a pause, at which he said nothing, I continued, "It's also important that the employees understand fully how this works, and it's equally important that they participate in this process. They should even be a part of designing the system."

"But you've already designed the system," he said, holding it in front of him.

"Greg, you're really on my case here. I'm surprised at your hostility toward all this. What you're holding is just an example, a pattern of what the elements should be."

He said he'd think about it. It took another several months for me to convince him, and then it proceeded only in stages.

I offer this story to illustrate how ingrained people's attitudes can be against anything that smacks of "corporate paperwork." I'm sure Greg, who had started his career in a large corporation, had at some point felt victimized by the corporate paper machine. I've felt that way also and by that measurement alone might have been expected to avoid these kinds of systems and procedures.

Why didn't I? Simple. I came to define them not as a way for the company to maintain control but as a tool to give people more understanding, more clarity, and more freedom. To put that another way, these systems can be used either as a blunt instrument to beat people around the head and shoulders (the old corporate way) or as a tool to fine-tune understandings and provide assurance (the servant leadership way). It depends on how the system is used and who is using it.

From time to time, I counsel people who have been fired. I can't even recall how many had no real idea why they were fired. They either didn't know they were supposed to do what they had been fired for not doing, or didn't know they were not supposed to do what they had been fired for doing. In many cases, these were good people who were doing the work; it just happened to be the wrong work.

> *These systems can be used either as a blunt instrument to beat people around the head and shoulders (the old corporate way) or as a tool to fine-tune understandings and provide assurance (the servant leadership way). It depends on how the system is used and who is using it.*

How could this happen? Most often it does not happen suddenly; people become involved in job functions that they know how to do, so they keep on doing those "comfortable" functions with little acknowledgment that the department or company has changed emphasis. No one bothers to tell them, and there are no systems in place to require such a review.

I recall a magazine graphic designer who loved to do illustrations, and he was good at it. The better he got, the more illustrations he did. After several years, the magazine underwent a visual style change that called for more photographs and fewer illustrations. Understand that the designer's primary job was graphic design, but he liked, and had become comfortable with, the role of illustrator.

In this case, he was not fired. After awhile the art director simply said to him, "You're busy doing what we no longer need done. You have to choose between design and illustration, and if you choose illustration, you'll have to do that somewhere else." The designer stayed in the job, but he felt somehow betrayed because someone had changed the rules on him. He never was content again in the job and left after several months.

Personal contact is good; personal involvement is good; but it is unfair to people's futures for them to be held hostage to personal understandings without a formal system of follow-up and review.

There are many systems available with accompanying instruction manuals and forms and so forth. If you put the emphasis on using them as a supportive tool, then it doesn't matter which you choose or what terminology you use.

Here is my description of the elements and how they should be used.

Job Descriptions

There's nothing complicated about the concept of job descriptions, but my observation is that the problem with job descriptions in most organizations is that they are not dynamic enough. The job descriptions seem to get cast in stone while most jobs are constantly evolving. I once did an exercise with one of my client company's departments. I photocopied the job descriptions within the department, then cut off the title of the job and the person's name, leaving only the list of functions. I coded them for myself, then passed them around and asked each person to choose the one that described his or her job.

Do I have to finish this story? The whole session ended in a laugh fest. The descriptions, which had been written years before and never reviewed, could hardly be recognized as describing anyone's job.

There are two stages in writing a job description. One is when it is written by the hiring manager before the interview process. This description works for the first year. Next, the job description becomes an annual document of joint authorship, written first by the employee, then discussed and reviewed with the manager. This means that, annually, both people agree that this is the job that's being done and the job that needs to be done.

A job description begins with a job title and a general paragraph describing the overall purpose and responsibility of the job, reporting relationships, or team memberships as appropriate. In constructing this paragraph, ask these questions: (1) Why does this job even exist? (2) What is it to accomplish generally? (3) What is its relationship to other jobs in the department, group, company?

Next is a list of job functions. These functions are general in nature without timelines or deadlines attached. Some may include such descriptors as "timely" or "in accordance with deadlines" or "as agreed upon with the manager or team members" and so on.

"General in nature" means that you should avoid listing functions that are temporary or time-limited. Such functions belong on the list of performance standards. (Keep reading.)

The job description, though dynamic in nature, should remain basically unchanged for at least two or three years unless there is a fundamental change in the organization and the need for this particular job disappears or requires a dramatic transition in function.

Performance Standards

The performance standards document is the most dynamic document of all and the one that directs each person's activities for a specific period of time. The primary author is the individual employee, and the process begins with a conversation, then progresses to writing, then discussion, perhaps more writing, and finally an agreement.

The initial conversation need not be long or complicated, although it will tend to be more comprehensive with a newer employee. If you've been through the process several times with a veteran employee, the conversation might boil down to a fifteen-minute exchange. Let's say the employee's name is Judy.

You start by saying, "Judy, are there any standards in addition to the routine ones that you have in mind for this year? Any special projects, for instance?"

Judy might have something in mind. It could be anything; a new product idea, a research project, a list of new customer prospects. It could be something that she has delayed until her first priority functions were fulfilled. Or she may have nothing other than to improve performance on the routine functions this year.

But you as leader have a voice in this as well. You might have a project in mind. But in the spirit of conversation, you should ask for her reaction and opinion as part of the process. Always remember that you should not push her into biting off more than she thinks she can chew.

The conversation might go like this:

"Judy, I've been thinking that we should investigate a niche that just might be right for us, and it's a niche I don't think the competition has considered. How would you like to look into that as one of your standards this year?"

She might respond, "I'm very interested in that area, as you know, but tell me how much time you think would be required and what the deadline is."

"If we're going to make an entry into that market, then I think we'll need a preliminary analysis by the beginning of the second fiscal quarter. If the analysis is promising, you might or might not be involved in the next step, depending on your interests."

"I really want to do this, but I know I'd need some freelance support on the fieldwork. Would I have a budget for that?"

"I'm sure you would if the niche looks promising enough. Why don't you think about this, look into it a bit, then give me a budget and timetable as part of your performance standards. Okay?"

Keep in mind that you should never suggest a project or a special standard that will intrude excessively into the basic job function reflected in the performance standards. On the other hand, this is often the way new projects, and new opportunities, get started. And in any discussion of performance standards, you should never fail to end with two comments: (1) "Now tell me what resources you'll need to do what you've agreed to do" and (2) "Tell me now if, or how, I can help you, and anytime during this period that you feel you need my help, please ask for it."

When I headed a major magazine group, we went through a very fertile and dynamic period of new magazine development. Almost all of that was done as volunteer work by people who simply were interested in new product development and saw an opportunity for themselves in working to bring a new magazine idea into reality. In several cases, the key volunteer ended up being the top editor or art director.

I always found that in discussing and negotiating performance standards, the really top people seemed to want to take on more than I often felt was reasonable, and I found myself holding them back a bit because there is ever the possibility that people will take on enough to hang themselves, and part of the servant leader's responsibility is to not let that happen, while at the same time, not repressing their ambition.

The other side of the coin is that people who are lesser performers frequently want a lower set of standards than you feel is required of a member of the group. In these cases, you try to gently negotiate more for them to do. This can be delicate, but it's also a responsibility of leadership and management to assure that each person is doing his or her share.

Of course, you can assign performance standards, but in the servant leadership workplace, it's better if the process is an agreement between employee and manager about what is to be done in this next time period and by what deadline it is to be done.

Let me be clear about what I mean by "agreement." It is not a contract with built-in provisions for enforcement, reparations, and so on. It's more like a covenant, a moral agreement between two parties, that these things will be done by the time agreed upon. This distinction is important because there must be flexibility for change, and employees cannot feel that they are being asked to write standards by which they may ultimately be hanged.

Performance standards derive from the job description but are not limited by the job description. They may include temporary or time-limited projects that are not mentioned in the job description and may not even fit under one of the general categories of the job description, though this would be unusual.

The standards state what is to be done, often also including a productivity standard, and a deadline by which it is to be completed. And they state in writing the basic agreement. In fact, I like performance standards to begin with this statement: "My performance will be judged satisfactory this year [or whatever the period may be] when I have done the following . . . ." The value in this should be obvious. There is assurance that no employee is in jeopardy of dismissal for failing to perform as long as these specific functions are accomplished.

For instance, let's go back to graphic design as an example.

The job description may say, "Designs pages for *BOB* magazine in accordance with design criteria established by the art director and in accordance with deadlines." That would be a fairly common sort of item in a job description.

The appropriate performance standard might then say, "Will design twenty pages per monthly issue for

BOB magazine in accordance with the art director's established design style for those issues. Will be completed by the tenth day of the third month preceding the on-sale date of the issue."

See how specific the standard is, and see how it is related to the job description? The "twenty pages" phrase sets both a performance and a productivity standard; the art director's design style establishes a quality standard; and the time factor establishes the per-issue deadline.

Now suppose this designer suddenly faces a highly complicated set of pages. Let's say that the editor of the magazine decided to do a special section involving drawings, items such as floor plans or three-dimensional drawings, or special colors or other design factors. It may become impossible to meet the productivity standard in such a case, even though there may be even more demanding work involved in designing fewer pages. But by the agreement, the designer's job is secured by the performance of the standards. Now what? As I said, in the servant leadership workplace, performance standards should be dynamic and can be subject to change and renegotiation in response to changing circumstances.

In this case, the designer talks to his or her manager, usually the art director, and says, "Look, this unpredictable situation means that I'm not going to be able to meet performance standard number one. I wrote that on the assumption that there would be no appreciable change in the way we designed the pages. I need to revise that standard to accommodate the changes in design requirements."

Because the performance standards began with a conversation and became an agreement, not a hard-and-fast contract, they are open to this kind of further conversation and review. The art director in this case may have someone else who can help take up the slack. This, of course, would mean that the art director would now have to initiate a conversation about performance standards with the other person.

Or the art director might ask the original designer, "What resources would you need in order to accomplish the original standard?" Perhaps the answer involves temporary freelance help. Whatever the solution, it would be worked out jointly, and the performance standards would be revised accordingly.

I've also seen situations in which the employee came to a point of having more time or opportunity to accomplish something in addition to the original list of standards. That, too, becomes a conversation and an agreement. The manager might have other ideas.

The point is that the employee always has a voice in the basic determination of what is to be accomplished in this job during this period of time. How long should that period be? There's no standard, though the most common practice is annual standards. It should be no longer than a year, but it could be quarterly or every six months depending on the kind of job.

Taken together, the job description and the performance standards become invaluable tools in two vital ways.

First, they absolutely require that there be communication between manager and employees. Even in a workplace that emphasizes open and honest communication, everyone can become so busy that important conversations keep getting postponed.

Next, these tools assure that all employees have a voice in determining what their job should be and what should be accomplished in a given period of time in order that the job be judged satisfactory.

"So," you may ask, "the job gets judged satisfactory. How about an above satisfactory performance or even an outstanding performance? Is everybody just satisfactory because they get the basic stuff done?" Good question (keep reading).

Performance Appraisals

When I started out in corporate life, there was no formal appraisal system. In fact, it was altogether difficult to figure out whether the boss was pleased with my work or not. I once asked him how I was doing and received an answer that I suspect was not uncommon in that day: "Just stick with what you're doing, Jim, and if you screw up, I'll let you know." It was like the old marriage joke in which the wife complains that the husband never says he loves her anymore, and he replies, "Look, if I don't say I don't love you, then I love you."

Things are generally better now, in that most companies, most organizations of all kinds in fact, have formal appraisal and review systems. But the system is only part of the point. As with performance standards, performance appraisals should be a tool of communication and should begin with a conversation.

(*Note:* For our purposes here, we assume that the standards were performed. Nonperformance is another subject to be covered in chapter 7.)

When I did these appraisals, I always sent a blank appraisal form to the employee several days before our meeting and asked that the employee do a self-appraisal using the company's numerical rating system. I said we'd then compare the two, mine and the employee's. It always fascinated me that the really top-performing people were more likely to give themselves a lower rating than I gave them, while the lesser performers usually rated themselves higher than I did.

I also asked that the employees come prepared to evaluate my performance in relationship to their job and to the goals of our department. It is not unique to ask for an employee's appraisal of your performance, but in the servant leadership workplace, there must be an absolute, inviolable understanding that the appraisal meeting is a "safe place," that there will be no retribution or negative reaction of any kind to the employee's honest appraisal, even if you heartily disagree with it. If you've not yet developed the temperament to handle this, keep working on it, but don't ask for the appraisal, because if you lose your cool only once, the employee will never trust the situation again.

The appraisal meeting is the manager's opportunity to formally assess how the employee has accomplished the standards of performance. It is at this point, as part of the conversation, that you as manager can say, "Yes, the standards were accomplished, but now I want to tell you my evaluation of how well they were accomplished, then get your response and go from there."

An important point: If your appraisal is greatly different from the employee's self-appraisal, then something's wrong. You probably have not done a good enough job of providing feedback (a machine word, I know, but useful in this context) throughout the year. The one formal appraisal a year is not enough, and if the employee gets a big surprise, this signals a failure to regularly communicate in order to give the employee a chance to make midcourse corrections. The appraisal does not substitute for the normal job of response and critique when you see that someone needs help in refocusing or redirecting.

> *An important point: If your appraisal is greatly different from the employee's self-appraisal, then something's wrong.*

The flight instructor analogy is useful here. Flight instructors spend most of the time teaching student pilots how to recover from hazardous situations such as spins and stalls, low fuel, forced landings, and instrument failures. The challenge for the instructor is to let the student replicate the hazardous situation then recover from it, but not let the student go so far as to crash. It is sometimes a tricky balance to maintain.

As a manager in the servant leadership environment, you can't be looking over people's shoulders. There's no empowerment in that. At the same time, you must also be sensitive to and aware of potential mistakes that could result in a negative appraisal or worse for the employee, and a possible threatening situation for the enterprise. Serving as a resource, being useful, is one of the characteristics of servant leadership; it is in that context that you make yourself regularly available to help employees perform as well as they can.

The final step in the appraisal process, depending on your system, is the rating. Some companies use words, some use numbers. In most cases, merit increases and other aspects of reward are tied to this rating.

I admit that it is philosophically troublesome that some people in a community of work, in somewhat comparable jobs, are paid more than other people or receive a higher percentage merit increase than other people. Once again, it's a balancing act because while there must be recognition and reward of the community's accomplishments as a group, there must also be the potential for individual accomplishment, recognition, reward, and advancement. I have seen some companies, particularly in the 1980s, try to establish only three or four grades of pay, then pay everyone within those grades the same, but I've not yet seen it work. And it strikes me as not only futile but also out of sync with the way employees expect and want their reward systems to work.

In summary, the challenges of the manager who would become a servant leader are no different from the challenges of any manager. How do you find and keep good people and make them productive; how do you train them in the ways of the servant leadership workplace; how do you achieve clarity about what is to be done; and how do you appraise and evaluate their performance?

There are no special tools and no quick and easy answers. Because the transition from management to leadership is a transition from the external (doing things right) to the internal (doing the right thing), the answers rest within you, and the efficacy of the tools depends not on the tools themselves but on how you use them.

CHAPTER SIX

Coping with the High-Tech Workplace

THE AGE OF ELECTRONIC assistants has brought convenience and productivity to the new workplace. No question. It has also often brought a preoccupation with technology to the extent that personal relationships have been neglected or ignored. And why not? It's far easier to deal with machines than with people. When a computer crashes, you can curse it or yell at it with no fear that it'll respond with anger or hurt feelings. So given a choice, many people would prefer to deal with the machine.

How does the servant leader respond to this trend? How does the leader maintain the focus on respectful human relationships, not on machines, as the central resource of an organization?

I offer for your consideration four myths which servant leaders must address if they are to bring human perspective to the excessive enthusiasm now surrounding the marvelous new technological tools:

Myth One: We are more connected.

Myth Two: All our electronic tools have made communication faster, better, and more accurate.

Myth Three: Having people come to a central place to work in groups is being made obsolete by the new tools.

Myth Four: When people multitask they get more done.

I realize that I'm committing heresy against the orthodoxy brought to us by the prophets of technology, but let's not forget that the prophets of technology are the ones most likely to profit from it. And like all prophets, their vision may be both accurate and distorted at the same time, accurate as to the facts of what is possible or likely, and distorted as to the truth of what is possible or likely. The first has to do with what the tools are technically capable of, and the latter to do with how people will choose to use those tools and the human impact of those choices.

Not that I am condemning technology and what the new tools have brought to all of us (yes, I use every one of the basic office electronics including a PDA, laptop, cell phone, e-mail, the Internet, and so on), but I believe that we've let our enthusiasm for these things make us forget that they are only that: tools. They are not the work, and they do not substitute for the work.

Substandard work done efficiently or committed to a slick PowerPoint presentation, illustrated by colorful graphs, photographs, and even video patches, is still substandard work. It falls into the same category with yesteryear's poorly written presentation that the writer thought he could make great by having it neatly typed and put in a ring binder.

The servant leader must create an ethic that honors work well done, not just a lot of work done.

So let's look at the myths one at a time.

Myth One:
We Are More Connected

Obviously we are more connected electronically, but the servant leader must recognize and embrace the paradox that, while becoming more connected electronically, we are becoming less connected personally. This is a particular challenge for a caring leader because it is within the confluence of human connection that the workplace is made habitable for the human spirit and that the work itself becomes a source of meaning in people's lives.

Years ago, a very prescient CEO warned me of the "tyranny of technology." At the time, I was about to commit millions of the company's dollars to a new and largely untested computer typesetting system for all our magazines. Clearly, the future required a computerized approach to processing the millions of words and thousands of images our magazines dealt with every year. A

HIGH-TECH WORKPLACE MYTHS

Myth One: We are more connected.

Myth Two: All our electronic tools have made communication faster, better, and more accurate.

Myth Three: Having people come to a central place to work in groups is being made obsolete by the new tools.

Myth Four: When people multitask they get more done.

task force group of our employees and managers decided that it should be sooner rather than later. In retrospect, I realized they had just become entranced with the technology without examining thoroughly the difficulties or the magnitude of such a transition.

I'm not sure it was a bad decision; on the other hand, the system created so much frustration that we actually had editors resign from the company rather than work with the system. All the while, the people who installed it and who maintained it and who provided the technical training kept blaming the problems on our editors and their inability to master computer typesetting.

It became abundantly clear that the technocrats believed in the system and its capabilities, while I knew our future depended on the creative people and their capabilities. It also was clear that the company that sold us the system failed to deliver on the hype, yet its representatives seemed to have co-opted our technical people into the deception.

"All these computer guys are in this together," I thought. "They think our people are here to serve the system and not the other way around."

I finally called them in and said, "Listen, folks, I respect your enormous knowledge and expertise, and I truly believe that in the long run, this system and other, more sophisticated ones will revolutionize the way we make magazines. But in the short run, these computers are frustrating and angering the editors and designers. And they, not the system, are the heart of our company. So you have to use your considerable know-how to make this a lot easier for them and on them. Take my word for this, folks, I'll move this whole group back to typewriters and copy pencils before I sacrifice any more good people on the altar of this system. Now tell me how I can help you help them."

We worked out a program for even more training, and we began to investigate other (and very costly) systems to make up for the original system's deficiencies. We chose people from the creative group who seemed to have a knack for the process, then included them as trainers so that the training would incorporate an element of peers helping peers rather than technicians instructing "creatives." It finally worked, but after much cost and who knows how many wasted hours and lost potential.

But this is not the real story. The real story is that the system became a flashpoint of discontent that made it very difficult to return our workplace to a creative and positive environment. It set up the conditions of competition and even hostility between our creative group and the technicians. I and other leaders put enormous emotional energy into restoring peace and creating a mutually beneficial environment.

This was my introduction to the "tyranny of technology," as well as a lesson in how difficult it is to impose a huge systemic change without doing the proper groundwork with the people who are to be most affected by that change. In recent years, I've seen this tyranny of technology still at work in large ways and small. And I've realized that leaders must embrace yet another paradox: They must seek the best tools as a resource for the employees while remaining wary about promises and expectations. As part of that paradox:

The leader must take an active role in evaluating proposed technology tools to assure that they will serve the employees in accomplishing their goals and the goals of the organization. Far too many leaders/managers buy into the promises of the technology vendor, then try to impose that on the employees. The employees should be included in any evaluation, either randomly or as an evaluation committee.

The leader must assure that people are given appropriate training, support, and encouragement. Believe it or not, there are still plenty of people in all kinds of organizations who are intimidated by the technology and by the pace of change.

Then the leader must keep the focus on the goals that the technology is intended to help achieve, and not on the technology itself.

The issue, becoming not only ever more ubiquitous but also ever more difficult for today's leaders, is whether we will become so obsessed with the glamour and glitz of all the new devices coming into our lives that we forget their basic purpose: to free us from the more mundane functions in our work so that we may bring our full creative energy and our full humanity to the task of doing our best work, with good people, in a community of effort that allows all of us to fulfill our purpose and the organization's purpose. That's what it really means to be connected.

Myth Two:
All Our Electronic Tools Have Made Communication Faster, Better, and More Accurate

Let me quickly say that these tools have made the transmission of information faster, better, and probably more accurate. But they have not done the same for communication.

Before you write me off as a Luddite about technology, let me relate a couple of experiences from the past few days.

A CEO client called me on his cell phone from an African safari. "I've been watching lions and elephants today, so I thought I'd call you," he said, laughing. He called specifically to get my reaction to the company's new booklet containing the vision statement, which is entitled "The Things That Matter." His company is located in Sydney, and he was on holiday.

I confess that I was impressed at the way technology has shrunk time and distance. That feeling was then emphasized a couple of days later when another CEO client called from his houseboat in Amsterdam. His company is in Boulder. What a world.

On the surface, those calls seem to affirm what I've called a myth, that our electronic tools have made communication faster, better, and more accurate. But while the technology involved in those calls certainly uses new equipment, it's nonetheless an old and well-tested paradigm: in a phrase, a phone conversation, and most of us have become pretty good at achieving a level of intimacy over the phone.

The problem rests, I believe, on the assumption that if we can just figure out more ways and more efficient ways to send words and images to one another, we have enhanced communication. To the contrary, communication is not an act, an episode, an incident; communication is a process that involves the active participation of both the communicator and the communicatee. What the technologies do is provide convenient ways to transmit information that may, and I repeat *may*, make communication easier or even more effective. But communication as a concept far transcends the exchange of information, just as truth far transcends accuracy.

A pet peeve and, I believe, a somewhat pernicious factor in organizational communications these days is e-mail. Think about it a moment: Has e-mail made for better communication in your organization? I suggest that e-mail is great for sending information but generally lousy for communicating.

> *I suggest that e-mail is great for sending information but generally lousy for communicating.*

In too many cases, e-mail has replaced the old ego memo. That was a memo written not to convey or seek information but to impress the boss. Frequently, before computers, the ego memo would be "carbon-copied" to a large list of people whom the writer was trying to impress. After the advent of the photocopying machine, this phenomenon became worse. And now, with e-mail, it requires only the push of a mouse button to send your e-mail to everyone in the company, whether or not they need or want to see it.

And e-mail has a disadvantage the old memo didn't: It's instant. A good piece of advice almost every new employee received only a couple of decades ago was, "If you write an angry or complaining memo, take it home, read it, and sleep on it before you send it."

Now it's *click* and there's no getting it back an hour later when you decide that perhaps you've been rash. I've been brought into companies to help resolve conflicts between employees whose sole "communication" with one another had been through heated e-mails. They weren't communicating at all; they were venting, maneuvering, trying to gain advantage. Only when I sat them down, facing one another, in a quiet room with no phones and no pagers, did they begin to communicate. This, of course, began to happen as a result of simply seeing one another as fellow human beings, not as screen names.

Finally, I have observed that e-mail has actually cut down on the time people spend together at the workplace. I've seen people send e-mails to a colleague in the next office rather than just poke their head around the corner and engage in conversation.

I know a manager who, when she wants some help or advice, now makes it a practice to walk directly to someone's office and ask for it. I know that her company discourages those kinds of ad hoc meetings and encourages e-mail, so I asked why she does it.

"Because I've learned that people get so many e-mails they tend to be out of sight, out of mind. They just forget the e-mails because there are so many. In fact, they forget your e-mail because they've probably filed it or deleted it and are reading someone else's e-mail. I've learned that the most effective way to get things done is to deal personally with the people face-to-face."

As for leaders, they must resist the temptation to become slaves to e-mail. I've heard too many management people complain about the number of e-mails they receive. "I don't even want to go on vacation," one manager told me. "My husband doesn't want me to take the laptop and work, but I know there'll be so many e-mails when I return it'll take three days to get through them all."

What a comment on how we've chosen to respond to all this "faster, better communication."

What is unsaid by that manager and others is that they are spending more time with e-mail than with people. If that is true for you, I suggest a drastic solution: First, declare a temporary moratorium, perhaps two weeks, on e-mailing you; next, define for yourself what kind of information you want to see on e-mail and what kind you don't; next, share this information as sort of an e-mail protocol for all your colleagues and employees; and finally, by all means have your name deleted from all those "all company" e-mail lists.

Believe me, more good ideas, better understanding, and more creativity come from personal contact than from blizzards of e-mail. More is communicated with a smile, frown, shrug, head shake, nod, or wave than from all those cute constructions of smiles and frowns you can devise on the keyboard with punctuation marks. :)

Nothing, absolutely nothing yet invented or to be invented, will replace those mystical moments when people meeting or just hanging out wander into someone else's office with a problem or an idea and, after periods of talking and silence and talking again, discover that a new idea, a better idea, or a solution reveals itself, magically, it often seems.

It is important for the servant leader to help people realize that communication results from human contact and that communication is not necessarily about words; it can just as easily emerge from silence, a gesture, a facial expression, even a sigh. And receiving this nonverbal communication is a skill that must be exercised and refined, particularly by anyone who aspires to become a leader. It can't be done electronically. Thus the leader must also provide opportunities, structured if need be, for people to spend plenty of what now is being called "face time" together.

Myth Three: Having People Come to a Central Place to Work in Groups Is Being Made Obsolete by the New Tools

I had a phone call recently from a former colleague who, seeing an opportunity a few years ago to market her skills as an independent contractor, had established and built a successful consultancy. I had seen her from time to time and had been assured things were working out well.

"I set my own schedule, and I've gotten to the point that I'm able to take the jobs I want and reject the others. I work with people I want to work with, and I can work in my pajamas if I wish."

"Sounds Utopian," I responded at the time.

"And I spend very little time in meetings," she added. "Remember all those meetings that wasted so much time? Well, I have none of those."

It was in the context of this previous conversation that I was so surprised by her recent phone call.

She began the conversation with friendly banter and exchange of small talk about family, friends, and so on. Then she turned serious and said, "Jim, I'm putting my résumé out there in the job market, and I want to ask if you'd let me list you as a reference."

"Of course," I said. "List me as a character reference as well as a professional reference, but . . ."

"I know you're wondering what this is all about," she interrupted. "First I want to say that my business is still going very well, and there are no family or financial problems. I just want to go back to a company, or nonprofit, or any kind of organization where people work together."

I said only, "I see," because I knew what was coming next.

She continued, "I'm tired of working alone all the time. I miss the people."

"Why?" I asked.

"Just the human contact for one thing, but more than that. I miss having people to bounce ideas off, have them bounce ideas off me. I guess you could say I miss the creative energy of a workplace environment."

I pushed a bit. "But you are well connected. You're in touch by e-mail and cell phone and fax and all the other things that allow for remote officing these days."

"It's not the same," she answered.

"Say more about that."

"Well, it's hard to explain, but there's just something about being able to stroll into someone's office and just start talking about a project or an idea or a problem, then as we talk, there begins to be a certain energy. Maybe someone else comes in and before you know it, we've solved the problem or come up with a better idea. Or something. As I said, it's hard to explain."

"I understand," I said, "but if you had to put it in one word, what is it that you miss most?"

"I guess I'd say the sense of community."

Exactly.

My friend John Naisbitt had it right some twenty years ago when he coined the phrase "high tech, high touch," suggesting that as our world evolved into a more high-tech environment, it required a more high-touch approach to customer service, employee relations, and so on. John was discerning a basic human need, I believe, and one that becomes more important proportionately with the development of our electronic tools.

This underlines the servant leader's most important role: community builder. People who are working together, performing their mission in order to fulfill their purpose, are in fact engaged in a community of work. This role was difficult for the leader even when people came together in a central place; it became more difficult with the development of remote or branch offices; and now it can seem impossible with the advent of "virtual offices," individual employees performing their jobs wherever they are, connected electronically without face-to-face contact with fellow workers or with the leader.

One of my clients, the president of a media company, as one of his first acts upon getting the job, identified the problems of the virtual office and its potential impact on the company.

"Our business is built on relationships," he told me, "so the whole notion that our field people operate almost as independent contractors is not acceptable."

"Why?" I asked.

"There are several problems. One is that as associates, as members of our team, I just feel they have to *associate* [he emphasized the word] with other company people, and they have to be *members* [he emphasized this word also] of something."

"But why?" I probed.

"Because without that association, that sense of membership in something . . . or to put that a better way, without a sense of belonging and participation in a group effort, the employee loses focus on what we're trying to accomplish together."

"So what?" I was pushing him, but he recognized it as such, and I could see he was pulling his reasons together for me.

"I think there are several negative results. For one thing, I think the quality of the work declines. For another, an employee will rarely innovate without being exposed to what others are doing. For another, there is the risk that the employee begins to think of himself or herself as separate from the company and becomes something of a cowboy or free agent, which in turn promotes turnover as that person is easily hired away. And finally, there is almost no opportunity for us in management to evaluate the employee's attributes on anything except technical competence and accomplishment; there's no chance to observe people skills or to determine potential for leadership."

He paused, then added, "You just can't build an organization with lone wolves. I just believe that everyone needs to feel personally involved with other people and with the organization. Not everyone would agree, I guess, but I believe it makes for better work."

I told him I agreed, then asked how he overcomes the lone wolf syndrome and how he deals with these scattered one-person virtual offices.

"I bring them here six times a year."

"That sounds costly."

"Most good investments cost something," he said, "and as long as I'm getting the results, I don't have to apologize to anyone for the legitimate costs of getting those results."

What my client was articulating, in so many words, was his belief in the community of work, in the power of people gathered together in a common endeavor. Communal work has characterized and indeed enriched human experience for centuries; it has been the source of ritual and celebration as well as sustenance. It would be foolish to think that somehow our new tools can replace the enormous creative and spiritual energy of people in relationship and in community.

So the servant leader's job is to assure that people working in the "virtual office" don't become "virtual employees" and instead are included in the community so that all may benefit. This may involve bringing them to the headquarters, as my client does, or visiting them regularly, making them part of a team that requires face-to-face gatherings from time to time, or organizing retreats and conferences, which may also be thought of as community celebrations. These gatherings are valuable resources in the leader's repertoire of community building tools. They are just as important, perhaps more so, than any computer, cell phone, pager, or PDA in the inventory.

Myth Four: When People Multitask They Get More Done

Let's start with the fact that people don't multitask; computers multitask. People may try to do two or three things at the same time and, depending on the definition of "do," may succeed to some extent. But they are not multitasking in the computer sense of the word.

In fact, I believe that the use of such words as *multitask, access, interface, download,* and others to describe human activity versus machine activity is one of the subtle ancillary aspects of the high-tech workplace that contributes to the further dehumanization of that workplace. Call me a language fanatic if you will, but words at their very best are filters we use to describe ideas, actions, and feelings. They can never be precisely accurate. But when we stoop to using machine terminology in the description of our human work, we subtly communicate the idea that we think of one another more as machines than as people, that we identify one another by our function, not by our personhood.

Just as troubling, we begin to think of ourselves in the same way. The servant leader must place a high premium on language because words are the basic tools of leadership. Your words as leader are more important than you can imagine. Ask yourself the question I frequently ask my clients: Can you remember a time when you were elevated to the heights of good morale or plunged to the depths by a casual comment your boss made? Everyone answers yes to this question. Let this be a cautionary guide about how you use language with the people in your care.

The emphasis on computer language can encourage nonproductive activity. Employees' belief that they, like computers, have the capacity to do more things at the same time can become, in effect, a way to avoid doing anything thoroughly or well. A CEO friend says this about multitasking: "It means that you are often screwing up several things at the same time." The leader has to be watchful about this. More important—to repeat myself—the leader must create an ethic that honors work well done, not just a lot of work done.

I did a management workshop recently for a telecommunications company. The venue was the company's conference facility. All participants had laptops and were networked. Several people clearly were more preoccupied with their laptops than with what was being said. At one point, I asked a young man if he was doing work not associated with the workshop subject.

"Yes," he said.

"I've tried not to be that boring," I said.

"You haven't been boring," he responded, "but I'm just multitasking. I work this way all the time."

What became clear, of course, was that he was not absorbing much from the workshop, and in turn, I doubt that he was getting much productive work done on the laptop.

I am reminded of what a business friend used to say about people who become enamored of their equipment and what it can do: "They are too preoccupied with their jobs to figure out what their work is. It's sort of like the race driver who has the best maintained and shiniest car, but he admires the car so much he can't pay attention to the race. The problem is, nobody will ever say, 'Old Joe never won a race, but boy did he have a great-looking car.' "

One of the most troubling trends in American work life is the inordinate number of hours that people seem to be working. I believe this trend is exacerbated by the siren song of technology that allows people instant access to their work, wherever they are, and seduces them into believing that the more they work, the more successful they will be. This then becomes an identity problem to the extent that some people can't feel worthwhile or useful or fulfilled if they aren't working.

A top executive told me in a private conversation, "I just don't relax well. I don't even know how to take time off." I don't think this is unusual among executives.

I don't know the solution to these problems, but I do know that this trend will ultimately be destructive for organizations as well as for the employees themselves.

The servant leader does not measure his or her success—or anyone else's—by the quantity of work done but by the quality of that work. The servant leader does not fall into the old-paradigm trap of evaluating people by the number of hours they work, whether they stay late or come in on weekends. Rather, the servant leader, out of the responsibility to be a resource and to serve, remains sensitive and aware of the impact of jobs on the individual lives of the employees. In addition, the servant leader assures that all jobs are structured appropriately (see chapter 5); emphasizes frequent critique, evaluation, and review to assure that what's being done is what's needed; and recognizes and credits effort but also focuses primarily on the results of the effort.

There's a good question to ask when responding to reports of such activities as "multitasking." The question is, "What did you accomplish?" When someone says something like, "I did this and this and this and this and this," you can respond, "I see you've been busy, now tell me what you accomplished." You may find that all that activity boils down to little more than the old military expression, "When in worry, when in doubt, run in circles, scream, and shout."

In the interest of not being misunderstood, I am impelled to say that the new workplace is exciting, stimulating, and dynamic. That energy is partly due to technology and its impact on the people. I repeat that I use many of the technologies myself.

But there is a seductive dark side that the leader needs to watch out for. The temptation is to believe that technology substitutes for good work or that it substitutes for human relationships. It does not. Technology is neutral; it can either enhance or distort the activities and relationships of the people. The servant leader's mandate is to assure that the machines are tools to enhance relationships and contribute to results that fulfill the people's and the organization's purpose—an old-fashioned use of the newfangled stuff.

PART THREE

The Harsh Realities of Organizational Life

THERE IS A JAPANESE riddle: "Who must do the difficult things?" Answer: "Those who can."

Even in a workplace characterized by the best principles and practices of servant leadership, there are people who do not respond, and there are problems that do not yield to the best efforts of the most evolved and advanced servant leader. It is with these people and against these problems that the servant leader must embrace the riddle's answer and become the one "who can."

I wish I were able to assure you that by embodying all the characteristics of servant leadership and by building a community of work based on the principles we've been discussing, you will never face the problems that every other leader faces, including the old top-down leaders. But it's not true.

Regardless of structure, of environment, or of leadership style, our organizations remain fundamentally human organizations, which means they will reflect both the strengths and the frailties of the human condition. There will be people who can't accept trust, people who prefer competition and confrontation to cooperation and consensus, and people who simply don't give a damn. There will be good, hardworking, and productive people who, through nothing but basic human circumstances, will face debilitating personal problems. There will be accidents, death, and disability of employees and their family members. There will be alcoholism and substance abuse. There will be inappropriate office romances. There will be sexual harassment. There will be personality conflicts. And there will be, yes there will most definitely be, lawsuits.

What I can assure you of is that in the servant leadership workplace, there is a greater possibility that professional problems and issues will be addressed with fairness and equity, and that the people are more likely to be supported as they struggle with personal problems.

It all depends on you. Your ability to face these perplexing and dispiriting challenges will be tested and will often strain your deepest reserves of emotional, psychological, and spiritual stamina. Leadership begins on the inside, with self-awareness and self-esteem, and the process of leadership involves regular and intense reflection and introspection. Without that knowledge of self, it would be impossible to manifest in these situations the sensitivity and responsiveness required of a servant leader.

For sake of discussion, I will divide these problems into three categories, though as you will surmise, there often is overlap. For instance, what begins as a personal problem may become a legal problem. What begins as an organizational action may cause personal problems. And so on.

Generally, however, it is helpful to think of these harsh realities of the workplace as falling into these three areas: organizational, personal, and legal.

CHAPTER SEVEN

Organizational Issues

ORGANIZATIONAL ISSUES INVOLVE SUCH things as negative appraisals, firings, layoffs, and structural changes.

I stress honesty as one of the vital characteristics of the servant leader workplace, yet I know that honesty is difficult to achieve. It's easy when we're passing out compliments—"Great job, Jim!" Nothing hard about that— but it's not so easy to say the negative things. Regardless of country or type of organization, I've found that the most widespread failing of managers at all levels is the inability, the unwillingness, the fear of saying, "Jim, you are not doing a good job," and then following through with a negative appraisal. I believe that most people want to do a good job and will do a good job if trusted to do a good job. That's the rule, but there is a corollary: Not everyone can accept trust, and not everyone wants to do a good job. I wish it were not so, but it is; and sooner or later, you will have to deal with some of these folks.

The Negative Appraisal

If you have established good systems, as described in chapter 5, you will have in place the foundation from which to proceed. But systems and procedures do not make any easier the personal part of the process. You must set a time and place and face a negative appraisal head-on, and you should not wait until the normal performance appraisal is scheduled. If at some point you see that a negative appraisal is coming, set a meeting time as soon as possible. Your ultimate goal is to give the person a chance to improve and to avoid probation or even firing.

The meeting does not have to be a confrontation, but be prepared for the fact that the employee will most likely disagree with your appraisal; some may even try to argue you out of it. I will never forget the time I gave a key department head a very negative appraisal. I'd done what I should in that I had critiqued his work regularly, assuring that he knew all was not well. So he came loaded for bear. As soon as I made my opening statement, he pulled out a ring-bound notebook, tabbed by performance standard, with lists of all he'd accomplished. I knew that his people had done most of the work and had carried him while he directed his energies toward personal projects, a serious failure on his part. And he knew that I knew, but he was determined to make our meeting as difficult for me as possible. I took the notebook, looked through it slowly and without comment, then said, "Joe, I think that if you'd put as much effort into your job recently as you've put into assembling this presentation, we wouldn't be here today." Then I put the book aside and continued with my critique.

Try to think of the negative appraisal meeting as "the caring confrontation" in which, no matter what the response of the employee, you must demonstrate that you're doing this because you care that the person is given as good a chance as possible to succeed.

> Try to think of the negative appraisal meeting as "the caring confrontation" in which, no matter what the response of the employee, you must demonstrate that you're doing this because you care that the person is given as good a chance as possible to succeed.

A good way to begin is by saying, "Joe, you are not accomplishing what we agreed upon, and the quality of your work is not up to our standard. Why?" Then be quiet. Even if the employee recognizes that you are probably correct, there still will be a certain degree of denial and defensiveness from most people. Believe me, it is rare for an employee to say, "Yeah, Jim, you're right. I've been doing substandard work, and I deserve to be given a bad appraisal."

In asking "Why?" you have directed the discussion away from whether or not the work is substandard and toward the reasons for it.

The employee's response can take many forms. Here's one: "I didn't know I was supposed to do that." Or, "I didn't know I was supposed to do it that way." At this point, the performance standards become your best resource because one of their most essential functions is to achieve clarity about what is to be done, how, and by what deadline. You simply remind the person that he or she is the primary author of this agreement, then ask again, "Why have you not been able to accomplish these?" or, if more appropriate, "Why are you doing this work in such a substandard way?" But do not keep talking. After you ask these "Why" questions, it's imperative that you wait silently for the answers.

Remain open to the possibility that there really is a misunderstanding or that more resources are required. If at all possible, you want to discover the reason and deal with it positively.

Here's another possible response: "I'm doing as good a job as Frank and Janet, and I have a larger workload than they do."

You can't allow yourself to be drawn into a discussion of other people's work or performance. The appropriate response is, "I can't comment on other people's performance. You'll have to trust me to evaluate everyone fairly, and right now that means we need to focus on your lack of performance. Tell me, why are you not doing the job?" Then wait silently for the answer.

In these discussions, it is important to be straightforward and focused, and it is just as important to remain calm, centered, and present. Don't allow yourself to be distracted by any interruption whatsoever; this should be an inviolable do-not-disturb event. Don't show agitation or anger, even though the employee may become heated and argumentative.

Be sensitive to the fact that in criticizing the person's work, you are often criticizing part of the definition of that person's self-perception. The work may be part of that person's identity, as it often is. Your words have the potential to do great emotional harm, and indeed you may at some

> *Be sensitive to the fact that in criticizing the person's work, you are often criticizing part of the definition of that person's self-perception.*

point in the process face tears and grief. If so, respond with affection, goodwill, and support. As I said in the previous chapter, the real difference between manager and leader is measured by the way these emotionally difficult situations are handled.

The negative appraisal is just that: an appraisal. It does not have to be the first step toward firing someone, though that may ultimately happen. Indeed, you should think of this meeting as a way to save the person's job, not to take it; thus, the meeting should end with a review of each performance standard to assure that it is still relevant. Rather than depend on the long-term deadlines of the standards, however, you should schedule a series of follow-up meetings, beginning probably at weekly intervals, then becoming monthly, at which both you and the employee will give a progress report. Your hope is that with this oversight and with appropriate resources, the employee will be able to turn in a satisfactory performance.

But it may not happen. Then comes a probationary period, once again with update meetings and deadlines, and once again with the goal of making the employee successful if at all possible, but with the realization that time is running out and that the next step may become inevitable.

Firing People

Firing people is a violent act. We'd like not to think of it that way, but in fact we are taking away someone's livelihood and are often delivering a terrible blow to the employee's sense of identity and self-esteem. As a manager and leader, you face the harsh reality that people have committed suicide after being fired; they have committed acts of violence against other people; they have fallen into substance abuse. It is in the contemplation of firing someone that the burdens of leadership reveal themselves most dramatically; it is at these times you recognize most acutely that the well-being of your employees is in your care during most of their waking hours. What a responsibility! That's why I refer to leadership as a sacred calling.

Firing an employee for lack of performance should be the last resort, but despite the moral concerns you feel in considering that act, it may be even a less moral act not to fire an employee for lack of performance. In the community of work, every person is important and every job is important; thus, the failure of one person in one job affects the entire community.

The dynamic tension that perhaps best defines the strength of our democracy is the tension between the rights of the individual and the rights of the group. Depending on who is in the White House or the Congress or the courts, the emphasis on individual rights or group rights shifts, relying on our systems of governance to maintain the tension and the balance.

But on the job, in organizational life, it is you the leader who must make that judgment call. You must decide when a person so abuses or misunderstands the goals of the organization and the understandings of the community—or is simply not competent to perform the job at hand—that the person can no longer be part of the group. On the one hand, your compassion and sensitivity will inveigh against the act of firing an employee; on the other, your moral responsibility to the rights of the group will demand that you do it.

It's easy to understand why so many managers over the years found it easier to fire someone in anger, but that is the coward's way out. Show me a tough guy who pounds the desk and yells, and I'll show you a coward who hides behind a shield of intimidation to avoid the truly tough stuff of acting with spiritual integrity and love.

Yes, I am saying that while people will never thank you for firing them—even though later they may even come to realize that it was for their own growth—you still can fire people with compassion, sensitivity, and understanding. Ultimately, firing a person who either cannot do the job, or does not want to do it for one reason or another, can be the most generous and loving thing you can do. But don't ever expect it to be easy.

As with the negative appraisal, you need to remain calm, centered, and focused, because if you've done what you should up until now, there is no turning back. You may be tempted because you'd like to be let off the hook as much as the employee would. But understand that normally you will already have heard of any extenuating personal or professional circumstances. So tempting as it might be, this is not the time for one more chance, for a little more time, for a reconsideration of any sort unless the employee reveals something that is truly unexpected and that in your judgment is so compelling it requires reconsideration. I emphasize that this will be very, very rare.

The actual procedure that follows the firing will depend on your organization's policies and procedures regarding length of notice, outplacement (if any), letters of reference (if any), severance pay (if any), and so on. Beyond that, here are a few general guidelines. (Keep in mind that we're discussing a failure to perform the job. Other reasons for firing, such as legal or ethical problems, will be handled differently.)

Within your policies, be as generous as possible with time and money. This is consistent with your servant leadership philosophy in that it is the most caring and supportive thing to do.

Allow the employee to participate in the wording of the announcement. If the employee would like to see it presented as a resignation, fine. I've seen too many of those cryptic announcements that so and so "is leaving the company to pursue other opportunities." That's code language for "We fired him," and everyone knows it. The pain is great enough without adding humiliation.

Avoid the "clean out your desk and be gone by five" syndrome. This employee failed to perform the job satisfactorily; presumably there's no suspicion of dishonesty, so give the person time to pack up, say good-bye to colleagues and friends, and depart with some degree of dignity.

These simple considerations not only are consistent with servant leadership but also will send a positive signal to other employees. Believe me, most everyone knows when a colleague is not up to the job; they won't be shocked by the firing, but they will notice how you handle the situation.

When in doubt, err on the side of generosity and dignity.

Layoffs

Layoffs are different from firings. The impact on the individual employee may be the same—loss of job, loss of income, loss of connection with the community of work—but for several reasons, the emotional issues are different for you as leader.

First, you are dealing with a group of employees rather than an individual.

Second, the reasons behind a layoff normally have nothing to do with competency or job performance but are related to overall organizational considerations.

Finally, in a large organization, you may not be the decision maker but simply one of the manager/leaders who must carry out the decision.

This doesn't mean that there is no moral issue involved. The question is not unlike the question of the rights of an individual versus the rights of the group. Although layoffs may happen for any number of reasons, they usually have one thing in common: They are intended to assure the long-term viability of the enterprise by eliminating operations that no longer contribute to the mission. Perhaps a business unit is not profitable; perhaps new processes have eliminated the need for its function; perhaps the organization has changed strategic direction. Whatever the reasons, they usually reflect the need to assure survival and future growth.

(It is true that in the eighties and nineties, some questionable layoff decisions [called "downsizing"] were made in the name of reengineering, efficiency, productivity, and so on, and resulted in wave after wave of displaced workers at all levels of companies. Most notably, this was the first postwar period in which white-collar, middle-manager employees were laid off in great numbers. No doubt some layoffs were necessary for the survival of those companies, but there's also no doubt that some were done because it became a management fad du jour, and because announcements of "downsizing" also always seemed to have a positive impact on stock price. I think this was a regrettable period and contributed to what is now called by many executives a "loyalty crisis" [see chapter 10].)

Assuming that you are considering, or are likely to be involved in a layoff, the moral question is simply this: "Will the survival and growth of the remainder of our enterprise be more likely assured by this action?" If the answer is yes, and assuming that all other alternatives have been examined, there is no moral alternative but to proceed with the layoff. It may be romantically appealing for everyone to struggle to the end together and all go down with the ship, all for one and one for all, but your responsibility as a leader requires that you act in the best interests of not only the employees but also the owners (stockholders), customers, vendors, and community at large. Absolutely no one would benefit from sacrificing the organization to avoid the pain of shutting down an operation and laying off employees.

So how do you do it? There's no one-answer-fits-all here because of differences in circumstances and organizations, but here are some general guidelines for the servant leader.

- Be sure that the first employees to know about the layoff are those who are to be laid off. That's primary.

- Then be open and honest with everyone, those who are being laid off and those who are not. Explain the reasons for the action, the difficulty of the decision, and the outcomes you expect.

- Honor the departing employees by expressing appreciation for their efforts. By no means should you ever put the blame on the employees; rather, if there is blame at all, direct it at the management or the market or other macro factors.

- Work within your system to arrange early retirements or other such arrangements if possible.

- Give first consideration for any existing job openings to the employees being laid off.

- In the policy areas of severance pay, outplacement support, continuation of benefits, and so on, be as generous as you possibly can. For an example of how one servant leader company handled a major layoff, see chapter 10.

Structural Changes

Structural changes may be related to layoffs in that jobs may be eliminated by such changes. These include reorganizations that in the normal course of events may be necessary from time to time as conditions change. Some operations within an organization may grow while others may stay the same or grow at a slower rate or even decline in importance and contribution.

One of the leader's primary functions is to assure that people have the resources they need to do the job. In a changing environment, the management, and sometimes reallocation of existing resources, is a constant imperative. This often requires that you be able to shift people from one department to another, that you cluster several departments into a larger group, that you do away with old structures and organize into teams, that you create time-limited task forces or working committees, that you group people by function or process rather than by product. How you may decide to use all the resources available is limited only by your imagination and your ability to inculcate these changes into the organization and the culture. The only requirement is that anything you do be driven by a clear definition of how it helps accomplish the mission in order to fulfill the organization's

115

purpose. Unfortunately, over the years, too many organizational changes have been made as ego trips only to reinforce the manager's position of power by maneuvering favored people into positions that will support that power.

Remember that anything you do is a change and that any change will be met with trepidation by some if not a majority of those to be affected. The old top-down way to make these moves is by carefully working them out, drawing up charts, calling a meeting, or sending a memo to spring on the employees. "Surprise! I've come up with a grand, new organization plan; now study the chart, see where you fit, and let's get to work."

The servant leader understands that nothing positive can be accomplished in an organization without the support of those who are to do the hard work. So, in contemplating organizational or structural changes, the employees—those closest to the process, the product, or the people (customers)—should participate in the decision. After all, they are the ones who'll have to make it work; thus, the major factor in making it work is their commitment. To paraphrase W. L. Gore, founder of Gore-Tex, productivity comes from commitment, not from control.

Of course, it would be more efficient to simply make the decisions and lay out the new plan for the group, but efficiency is often the enemy of effectiveness. What you desire is a result that will be effective in the long run, not efficient in the short run. So take the time to give everyone a voice in the plan.

Begin by setting forth the goals and the desired results of the reorganization, showing how those will enhance the group's ability to accomplish its mission. Then ask the people how they think these results might best be achieved and, if organizational changes are required, how might those look.

A few years ago, I worked with a company that had several different media products in the same general industry. The sales and marketing groups of each product were organized vertically in that each had its own sales director, sales manager, and individual salespeople. The result was that an advertising director of a client company might be called on, and hear a pitch from, several different salespeople from this same media company. There were complaints from the ad directors, who would call the president of the media company and ask, "Why do I have to listen to six different people? Can't you send one person to tell me about your company's products?"

> *The servant leader understands that nothing positive can be accomplished in an organization without the support of those who are to do the hard work.*

This question was simple enough, but what the ad director was suggesting would involve an almost revolutionary change in the sales structure of the media company. Not only would the sales effort need to be reorganized into category teams, but the whole compensation and incentive scheme would require an entirely new and untested approach.

Yet the ad director's question was compelling because within its call for more sensitivity to the customer's time, there could also be the opportunity to leverage more business from individual advertisers by packaging the media company's products into one sales proposition. In effect, there could be a volume discount for advertising in two or three or four or five of the magazines or Web sites. This could represent an even more efficient and effective use of the customer's time as well as of the sales force's efforts.

The more the company president and his senior management group thought about it, the more attractive the idea became. They began to envision how it might work, what the organization might look like, how the reporting relationships would work, and so on.

At that point, I said to the president, "It's time you started sharing this information and asking the advice of the people who would have to make it work."

His reply was that the whole proposition was so complicated it would be best in his judgment to draw up the plan, lay it out for everyone, and then get their advice.

"Sounds good on the surface, Mel, but in that case, you're not asking for their advice and ideas so much as you're asking them to critique what you and your management group have already done. And if they're brave enough to critique your plan, the predictable result is that when they do so, you or some of your people will feel so proprietary about all the work you've put into it that you'll begin to defend your plan rather than listen for a better way."

"But, Jim, what you're suggesting will take forever."

"I don't think so," I said. "I believe you can have a good plan, with everyone's support and buy-in, within three months. And this is something you won't want to put into effect until the next budget year anyway."

He agreed, though somewhat reluctantly. "How shall we begin?" he asked.

"Tell them that you've been thinking about the possibility of a more effective organization, that you started thinking about it because of the question this one big customer asked about why so many people call on him. Be honest in telling them that you and the management group have discussed this, but that now you've called all of them together to think about the following question: 'How can we serve our customers better?' "

He was startled. "Don't you think I should at least tell them what we've been thinking?"

"No, I don't," I said. "They're no fools. They know you have some ideas about it, but as soon as you tell them your ideas, they're not likely to put their own on the table. Listen, even if you've thought through every detail and are ready with the most efficacious solution, they will still feel it's being imposed upon them. It's only natural."

So he agreed. He told them what the ad director had suggested and simply asked the question, "How can we serve our customers better?"

To make the long story short, the final plan did not mirror what the senior managers had come up with, but the people were committed to make their plan work. And so far, it has. Furthermore, the company has been able to start other products without having to staff them from scratch with individual sales directors, sales managers, and so on; with only a few additions to staff, the new products were simply plugged into the sales structure and added to the media list.

This example was of a major change, but even smaller changes should involve in the decision making the people who are most directly affected and upon whom success depends. A good friend, CEO of a major financial company and a real servant leader, told me that while he knew the company's office hours needed to change to serve the customers better, he did not mandate it. He simply kept asking the question, "How can we serve our customers better?" and finally someone said, "Why not change our office hours?" He smiles with satisfaction when he tells the story because he enjoys the paradox that the most efficient thing to do would have been the least effective thing to do.

CHAPTER EIGHT

Personal
Issues

LAST YEAR, WHILE I was counseling a young information services manager in a rapidly growing company, he said, "The machines are so much easier to deal with than the people." He was feeling and expressing the frustration of many people who, because of their outstanding technical skills, have been thrust into supervisory or management positions with little or no training.

These new managers quite naturally assume that what they should do is make sure their employees strive for the same level of technical expertise and productivity that they themselves have demonstrated. They think the management job boils down to setting the example: "Hey, watch the way I do this, then do it that way, and you'll be successful." It does not occur to them that their new job will require not only technical expertise but also strong interpersonal skills and, in the case of servant leadership, the powerful personal characteristics of compassion, sensitivity, and humanity.

This is not a new problem. I personally have taken some of the world's best salespeople and promoted them into being among the world's worst sales managers. Not only did I not equip them adequately to do the technical stuff of management, the nuts and bolts of chapters 3–5, but more important, I did not prepare them for the emotional and spiritual challenges they would face. Yet it is here, in the deeply personal aspects of leading people, that the precepts of servant leadership are most necessary and, yes, most difficult to manifest.

There's no purely logical place to begin, but in my experience the following problem areas seem to be the most common in most workplaces: sickness and disability of an employee; sickness and disability of family members; alcoholism and substance abuse; inappropriate romantic behavior between workers; and sometimes resulting from the romantic behavior, sexual harassment.

Sickness and Disability

The sicknesses or disabilities (and sometimes both) of employees most often are temporary episodes that do not appreciably disrupt the flow of work or the workplace environment and should be addressed technically by the policies of your organization. In addition, I believe you should do the normal human things you might do for any friend or family member, the things that seem easy and natural: offer support, send words of comfort and encouragement, and so forth.

But what about the longer term problems, the illnesses that lead either to death or to long-term disability? Not only do these have a devastating impact on the lives of the individual employee, family members, and fellow workers, but they also are painful and spiritually debilitating for you as a leader. Anyone who has been in a leadership position for any length of time has faced these situations and has asked, "What should my personal response be?"

The answer should always begin with the desires of the employee. I have rarely seen a person who wants to take the company benefits and just be left alone to fight the fight and face whatever there is to face. If that is the employee's desire, respect it, but most often that is not the case. Over the years I've been astonished by how many people who have been struck with a life-threatening or even a terminal illness want to stay on the job and keep working. It's not about making as much money as possible at full salary before being forced into disability pay. Not at all. It's about meaning. It's about everything the servant leader feels and tries to create about the community of work: It is within what we have chosen to do and how we have chosen to do it that we find so much meaning in our lives.

People do not want to so easily let go of that meaning. Years ago, one of my employees, a good friend, was stricken with cancer. In asking to stay on the job, he put it this way: "Jim, I honestly feel that the longer I keep working, the longer I'll live even if I'm not cured." I agreed with him. He lasted about six months, but he did some important things in those months, and I know he derived great satisfaction from them. Also I felt most palpably his gratitude at having been given the chance to continue working. At the same time, I had to face some very difficult considerations.

I guarantee you'll have to face similar ones at some point in your leadership journey. Here are the issues: Do you let a sick employee (noncontagious of course) remain on the job even though you know that the work may fall below the normal standard or that the person's productivity will drop? How do you measure, and respond to, the reaction of the other employees, and just how much accommodation do you make in the name of humanity without imposing a burden on them? They probably will be sympathetic, but what do you do about the very real morale factor of coming to work with a dying person every day? From the viewpoint of your management responsibility to the organization, how much are you willing to risk a drop in productivity by all employees as they watch another human being fade further toward the inevitable deadline? We are all dying, of course, at one rate or another, but what is the impact of forcing employees to face their own mortality so dramatically every day? And what about the legal risks of a sudden change of condition in an environment not equipped to deal with it?

I wish I had hard, specific answers to all these questions, but I don't. And you won't either. Clearly you have an organizational responsibility and you have a leadership responsibility to the people. In the many similar situations I've faced and in the ones I've counseled leaders about, I chose to put the organizational responsibilities last on the priority list and the personal ones first.

The personal responsibilities are in two areas: the sick employee and the other employees. Between these two, I have always put the sick employee's needs first. My reasoning is that this person probably will never be cured from this terrible disease, but healing is not the same as curing, and all of us can have a role in the healing. To the extent that continuing to participate in the community of work is part of that healing, then we should make it possible right up until the point that the employee decides that functioning in the workplace is no longer possible.

As for the pain and morale problems of the other employees, I reason that I must be sensitive, counsel with them individually as appropriate, and be open to anything they want to say about the situation. But I reason also that they will still have an opportunity to heal from their own pain after the sick employee is past the point of healing. I've also been prepared to bring in professional counselors to help employees deal with death in their midst, but I've never had to do this.

As for the organizational responsibilities, there clearly could have come a point at which morale had such a depressing effect on productivity that it began to threaten the group's ability to achieve the results required. There are only two responses: Appeal directly to the employees to turn their attention to the work at hand, telling them that continuing to do good work is the best way to support their sick colleague; bring in counselors if need be.

But this can fail. And people will sometimes surprise, even shock you. In one case involving a person who chose to keep working after a diagnosis of terminal cancer, an employee of that department visited me one day.

He began the conversation by asking about the colleague's condition and what I planned to do.

"I hope to let Jane stay on as long as she wishes, though I know it's a tough situation."

"Worse than that," the employee said, "this situation is bringing us all down. I mean, we walk by her office and she looks awful, so we start tiptoeing around and being quiet, and the whole energy of the place drops."

"Have the others asked you to talk to me?"

"No," he said, "I took it on myself to come here because I think you need to know what's going on over there."

I was becoming very concerned by this conversation until he added, "When you do decide to send Jane home [his very words], I'd like to be considered for her job."

It was difficult to maintain my equanimity because I had a vision of the vultures circling, but I told him I'd think about it. After talking with a few other employees in the department, I decided to support Jane as long as I could. (It's not relevant to this story, but the man who came to see me decided after a few months that he'd rather be in another company.)

This story could have turned out differently. Jane's situation could have had such a depressing effect on morale and productivity that I might have had to "send her home."

In a similar situation, you would have no choice but to arrange disability leave for the sick employee, in accordance with the policies and procedures of the organization, and hope that, in the employee's absence, you could lead the workplace back into a normal working environment. I've never had to do this because in my experience, the affected employee always chose to quit working before the impact on morale reached a critical point. I can imagine that telling an employee that he or she could no longer hold the job and would have to now accept disability or sick leave would be far and away more difficult than firing someone. I can only suggest that it be done with as much sensitivity and dignity and love as possible.

Family Sickness or Disability

The sickness or disability of an employee family member is not as difficult a personal situation for you, but the servant leader should go beyond the official policies regarding family leave and support the employee as much as possible. Obviously, we're talking about longer term episodes, not the usual bouts with colds and flu that everyone faces from time to time.

In teaching new manager workshops, I like to ask this question: "Suppose you have an employee with a sick or disabled child, and in order to see to that child's needs, the employee will need special accommodations such as flexible hours, plus will occasionally on short notice need to go home. Now do you as a manager, perhaps with children yourself, support that employee as fully as possible, stretching the policies perhaps, caring about and nurturing that employee, doing everything you can to make this situation work for the person and for the company—or do you take the attitude that, 'Well, I have children myself, and I feel bad about this situation, but we've got to get the work done around here.' Which?"

It's a trick question. The constant reality for leaders is that they must embrace paradox. They don't live in a black-and-white, either-or world; they live in a gray, both-and world. The answer to that question is, "Both." And servant leaders embrace the paradox; they know they have to be nurturing and caring and supportive to the greatest extent possible, and they have to get the work done.

So in cases involving illness and disability in an employee's family, the servant leader must remain focused in three areas at the same time: what will work for the employee and his or her family; what will work for the other employees; and what will work for the organization.

Step one is to work with the employee to determine what special accommodations are required in order for the employee to fulfill the family responsibilities. Assuming that an extreme change is not needed, such as working at home full-time or working at times when no other employees are in the workplace, try to work out a schedule that will give the employee a chance to accomplish the performance standards and achieve the results while providing the flexibility to be at home (or wherever the situation demands). There may be no way to do this. If not, then try to accommodate the employee's needs for a specific period of time while helping him or her get placed in another job that better suits the required schedule.

> *In cases involving illness and disability in an employee's family, the servant leader must remain focused in three areas at the same time: what will work for the employee and his or her family; what will work for the other employees; and what will work for the organization.*

Even after working out an accommodation, there may come a point at which it is so intrusive into the flow of the workplace that you can't fulfill your responsibilities to the other employees or to the organization. The important thing is to do everything possible to avoid putting the employee on the street without income or benefits and facing a difficult family situation.

I have been involved in many such special arrangements, both as a leader in a corporation and as a consultant to senior managers. There's a trite old saying that fits most of the cases I've seen: "Where there's a will, there's a way." And another thing: Employees who have been accommodated in such a way become the most dedicated, committed, hardest working, and productive people you can imagine.

What about the impact on the other employees? A common question is, "Once you give someone special treatment or a special accommodation, then you're changing the rules and not treating all employees equally, right?"

The point is not to treat all employees equally but to give all employees fair and equitable treatment. People have different needs and even different work styles. Some people are great in the morning but their productivity drops in the afternoon; some do better on one kind of project than another. Whether we want to admit it or not, we as leaders are responding to special needs and circumstances all the time, and well we should, because if our job is to give people the resources they need and to assure the environment and conditions in which they can do their best work, then we should abandon the myth that all employees can be treated equally. In fact, equal treatment may often be unfair treatment. This is the rationale behind accommodating people with special family circumstances.

But remember this: You are accommodating needs, you are not lowering standards. This can be tricky, but it is important to be clear: Your special treatment of an employee must be accompanied by the understanding that you expect performance of the standards, both in quality and quantity as agreed upon. In this, you are putting the emphasis on results rather than work style, office hours, or any other such discretionary matter.

As for the other employees, be open and honest about the arrangements and about the expectations for performance. There may be those who will grouse a bit, but most employees will appreciate what you're doing and will realize there may well come a time when they'll have sickness or disability in the family, and they'll be reassured that their leader will be willing to accommodate them as well.

> *If our job is to give people the resources they need and to assure the environment and conditions in which they can do their best work, then we should abandon the myth that all employees can be treated equally.*

Alcoholism and Substance Abuse

The issues of alcoholism and substance abuse are related to sickness and disability but, while they require the same compassion and sensitivity from you, they require a different leadership response.

I got to the point in my career that I felt that alcoholism was an occupational hazard of the business. Those were the days when three-martini lunches and cocktail receptions were the venues for much selling and deal making.

I dealt with many cases of alcoholism among my employees through the years, but it was not until the seventies, with a different generation, that other forms of substance abuse entered the picture. I recall conversations with fellow senior executives in which we discussed how to deal with the abuse—or more accurately, suspected abuse—of illegal drugs. Should we treat it as an illness like alcoholism, or should we treat it as a legal issue?

There were opinions on both sides, but I came down firmly on the side of treating all substance abuse as an illness/disability issue. My feeling was that I was not in the law enforcement business, and while I felt we as citizens should cooperate and support law enforcement officials, we should not treat our employees as criminal suspects. Rather, we should treat them as people who need help. I think contemporary management practice for the most part embraces this approach.

And this is surely the way that servant leaders should think of substance abuse: placing the employee at the center of concern, with the objective being to help that employee get well and become productive again. However, your focus on treatment does not relieve you of the difficult caring confrontation.

Organizational policies and procedures may vary, but within those considerations, your leadership responsibility is to confront an employee who you are certain has a problem. But how? You can't say, "Jim, you're a drunk." Or, "Jerry, I have reason to suspect that you're a pothead."

No, your starting point is the job, the performance standards, the workplace relationships. I recall vividly a conversation I had with one of my senior managers who, obvious to everyone but him—which is usually the case—had become alcohol dependent and needed treatment. I knew that I could not take the role of doctor or therapist but had to approach him strictly as his manager.

I knew that his habit was to come in late, work until lunch, drink heavily at lunch, then work until cocktail hour. I knew also that his afternoon work time was fairly worthless to his group and to the company. I set a meeting with him deliberately right after lunch, thinking I could most dramatically make my point to him after he'd been drinking.

But he was a smart and clever guy—why else would he be working for our company?—and he had surmised that something was wrong, so he showed up sober and alert.

I began the conversation by asking, "Charlie, why do you suppose that no one in your group wants to schedule a meeting with you after lunch?"

"That's not true," he said, "I have meetings after lunch all the time."

"Meetings that you schedule or that other people schedule?"

"Both."

"That may be true, but I think if you'll check your appointment schedule, you'll find that you've scheduled what few after lunch meetings you have yourself. But that's not really the point, is it?"

He was silent.

"Charlie, I hope you know that I like and support you, that I think you have been one of our finest managers."

"What are you leading up to, Jim? Are you firing me or something?"

It would be very unusual for someone who was accomplishing the basic performance standards and who had a good record to suddenly jump to the conclusion that he was being fired. But I found this kind of suspicion and paranoia to be a common reaction of people I was confronting about substance abuse.

"No, not firing you, but something else. Charlie, it has become obvious to me and your colleagues and employees that you have a drinking problem, and that's what we're here to talk about."

He became angry and hostile immediately, though I don't think he was surprised in the least by the subject of our conversation.

"Like hell," he said. "Are you calling me a drunk?"

"Is that what you'd call someone who comes in late, drinks through lunch, is so unproductive and unresponsive in the afternoon that people avoid him, and who rushes off for a drink on the way home?"

"Who avoids me?"

I let his anger continue because I wanted him to blow off some steam and get worked up. I continued, "Charlie, if you didn't know in your heart that there is truth in what I'm saying, you wouldn't have such an overreaction."

"Overreaction? You tell me I'm an alcoholic, and I'm supposed to sit here calmly?"

"No. You're reacting exactly as I expected. Now let's get down to business. I'd appreciate it if you wouldn't say anything until I've finished telling you what your options are."

He nodded. His face fell, and I knew then that he was giving up the fight. He was an experienced enough manager to know that I'd have my say, then he could react, but he'd also have to make a decision.

"First, Charlie, you don't have to admit to me one way or another about the alcoholism. What I'm saying is that your work is suffering and your professional relationships are suffering, and I think it's because of your drinking. Regardless of the reason, your work is not acceptable.

"But because I think alcoholism is the primary cause, I'm making the following offer: The company and I will support you fully in a treatment and rehab program. We'll pay for it, and we'll give you time to do it. That's your first option."

"What if I disagree and don't think I should get treatment for alcoholism? This is not that big a problem; I can work it out on my own. I can cut back on my drinking anytime I want." (They all will say this.)

"Sorry, if you don't take option one, you're going to have to find a job somewhere else. That's the second option and the bottom line."

If you have been involved in persuading a friend or loved one to go into alcohol or drug treatment, you will recognize what I did as an "intervention," in which the options are laid out and a bottom line established. My friends who specialize in this kind of treatment tell me it's the most effective way to get someone into treatment. Alcoholics or addicts will rarely choose treatment because of the high level of denial they have about the problem.

On the surface, this action seems harsh rather than loving and supportive; it seems antithetical with the precepts of servant leadership. In fact, I can assure you that every fiber in my body wanted to give Charlie another chance, to let him work it out on his own, but it would not have been effective. You have to look beyond the initial conversation toward the desired outcome; the longer view is the more supportive and loving view.

There is no difference in the way you would do an intervention for any kind of substance abuse. Confront the person. Invite disagreement if the person wants to disagree. But put the job on the line. Treatment, with our full support, or out you go. Once again, you must stay focused in three areas of critical concern at the same time: the employee, the other affected employees, and the organization.

Charlie's story ended well. He went into treatment where every day as part of a twelve-step program he had to introduce himself by saying, "I'm Charlie, an alcoholic." When he told me the story of his continuing recovery a few months later, it was a very moving experience for both of us. I had felt just awful forcing him to choose between treatment or the street, and it was a very affirming experience to have him come into my office, give me a hug, and thank me. The last time I saw him, he still referred to himself as a "recovering alcoholic."

Office Romances

Some companies forbid office romances and will fire anyone caught "fraternizing," whatever that means. Other companies prohibit the employment of both husband and wife; thus, if an office romance results in marriage, one or the other will be fired. I think these policies are nonsense, out of touch with the real world while pretending to be "real-world tough," and clearly in violation of the precepts of servant leadership.

Just what is the problem with office romances? I am compelled to say that, assuming the affection is mutual, office romances need not be a problem at all and probably deserve only your benign neglect. (Disclosure: I met my wife at the office.) But they can become a problem under certain circumstances which you, as leader, will not be able to ignore.

In the normal pattern of responsibility, which I've mentioned several times, your concerns are always three: the employees involved, other affected employees, and the organization.

You are not, and should not try to be, the morality police, so even if a romance involves people who are married to others, your focus is not on the fact of the romance but on the behavior of the participants and the impact on other employees and the organization.

Here are some situations in which you must act:

- The participants may become so preoccupied with one another that they begin to ignore their work, which may decline in quality or quantity and not meet the standards.

  Your intervention in this situation takes the form of a negative appraisal, focused on the work and not on the behavior. You do not say, "Joe, you and Mary are spending so much time at coffee breaks or talking to one another in the office that your work is becoming unsatisfactory."

Rather, you say, "Joe, your work is sliding toward the unsatisfactory category. Why?" The old "Why" question again. This should lead to a discussion in which you can make the point that Joe doesn't seem to be putting the time and effort into the job, but you still should not refer to the romance. Joe knows why, and he knows that you know. If Mary's work is also declining, you should handle it the same way.

This is not rocket science; it just requires that you act forthrightly and make sure that Joe and Mary know there will be consequences of not meeting the standards.

- The participants may be inappropriately open in their displays of affection. Although the rules of romantic propriety seem to have all but disappeared from the media and from pop culture, they still are relevant in the workplace. The guideline is simple: Treat one another professionally in the workplace and save the heavy loving for another environment. Am I saying to prohibit physical expressions of affection in the workplace? Not at all; I'm saying to use judgment. There's a difference between a hug or a good-morning peck on the lips and a body-grinding embrace or a lingering kiss on the mouth. Your standard should be the standard that does not offend another worker.

Listen. I worked for a midwestern company employing many midwesterners among our diverse group of people, which also included younger writers, designers, illustrators, and editors from all around the country. These young people were not known for their inhibitions, but a lot of our older workers, many of whom were midwesterners, a group known for its reserve and stoic behavior, would have been offended by hand-holding or walking arm in arm. And if they'd been offended, they would have been distracted from their work. It would not have been good enough for me to say that they should just mind their own business and ignore what goes on around them. And calling it to the attention of the lovers, putting it in terms of those offended workers, usually solved the problem.

- One participant in the romance may cool to the relationship while the other may want to hold on. Man, can this get sticky, but your role is to keep the participants focused on their jobs and their behavior while on the job.

  I once failed to intervene soon enough in a situation like this, and before I knew it, the whole place seemed to be caught up in this real-life drama. It became the workplace soap opera. Both the man and the woman had their stories and their audience, and it seemed there was far more interest in the narrative of this failing love affair than in our collective professional narrative.

I called them both into my office. I was not harsh because I knew their crisis was real and that their feelings were legitimate and deserved to be addressed with sensitivity and dignity.

"I'm not a counselor or therapist," I said. "I'm your manager. I want to be sensitive to the pain and upset you're going through, and I urge you to seek whatever help outside the office that you need, but here's my professional analysis of the situation. Your behavior has become very distracting. Your fellow employees are all caught up in your love life, and it is becoming an organizational problem of morale and productivity. So here are your choices: Put your heads down and get back to work and save the conflict and discussion for after working hours, or I'm going to have to transfer one of you to another department or, if no other position is available, one of you is going to have to leave."

In any scenario in which undesirable behavior is caused by personal situations in which you have no legitimate role, your involvement must be work-related, and your only ability to bring about a substantial change in behavior is to resort to the bottom-line approach similar to a substance abuse intervention.

I ended up transferring one of them to another department.

Sexual Harassment

Sexual harassment is as contrary to the honesty, integrity, and mutual respect of a servant leader workplace as any behavior I can think of. Sexual harassment is not about sex; it's about power, and despite popular movies and stories to the contrary, men are the aggressors 90 percent of the time.

There are laws defining sexual harassment and prescribing what a company's response should be. How you respond to complaints of sexual harassment will depend first on your organizational policies and how strict an interpretation of the law they require. Some organizations mandate that any report of sexual harassment, no matter how informally reported or how insignificant it may seem on the surface, must be handled immediately and in a strictly legalistic fashion. In today's social climate, this "zero tolerance" approach is probably the safest way to respond. If this is the case in your organization, the events are usually prescribed, and there's no deviation from the procedures. All you can do is try to be sensitive to the people involved as the process unfolds.

If your organization allows you to use discretion as to the severity of the problem and empowers you to make some inquiries on your own, the first step is to talk with the person making the complaint. Your intention is to determine whether the harassment has reached the point of abuse, to get clarity in your own mind about what happened, whether it has ever happened before, whether there is a pattern of harassment episodes, and so on. It's important to determine whether the person making the complaint was personally and directly harassed or if she is responding to what is called "a hostile environment" or an "environment of sexual innuendo" in which she may be responding to a calendar or piece of art or a tastelessly sexist symbol of some sort. If there has been direct harassment, then the likelihood of abuse is much greater; in this case, I suggest you seek help from your HR department or from your legal department. There are specific steps that usually must be taken as a response.

If the issue is one of sexual innuendo or hostile climate, such as a photograph or even an off-color joke, you have more flexibility. Understand that these are not frivolous matters, however, and you must take them seriously. The courts have held that you simply must make a reasonable attempt to intervene to stop the harassment and to prevent abuse. If you do that and if indeed the harassment stops, that should be the end of it.

These days, most organizations provide regular training about sexual harassment, its definitions, the legal implications, and the remedies. But I recall several years ago when sexual harassment was first receiving its deserved attention as a workplace problem, there was in my group a young manager who took two women's shoes and placed them under his desk in a sexually suggestive position. This was in a branch office where senior management people like me appeared infrequently. It was reported later that most people laughed at this childish little joke, but one young woman complained to me. She was offended and upset. "Would you feel the problem was solved if the shoes were removed?" I asked.

"Only if he didn't do something like that again. And if you didn't have to tell him that I was the one who complained."

"In this case, I can honor that confidentiality," I said.

So I called him on the phone. "Mitch, are you sitting at your desk?"

"Yes," he said.

"Look down. Do you see two women's shoes arranged somehow?"

"Yes," he laughed, thinking, I suppose, that I appreciated the joke. "How did you know?"

"Never mind. Now reach down, pick up the shoes, put them in the bottom of your wastebasket, cover them with wastepaper, and leave them for the custodian to remove and throw away."

"What?"

"And use your head, Mitch. Didn't it occur to you that not everyone would appreciate that little piece of high school humor? You're a manager trying to become a leader. Part of that process is, as the doctors say, doing no harm. Anything involving sexuality or sexual innuendo has the potential to do harm. In addition, you have put yourself and the company in legal jeopardy, enough so that you could even have lost your job. You've had the laugh, now throw the shoes away, and use this as a lesson about unintended consequences."

I paused, then said, "I'm not angry and you're not in trouble, but it could have been serious." Then I explained the law on sexual harassment and the part about hostile workplace and sexual innuendo, and closed by asking, "Do we need to discuss this any more?"

"Nope," he said. "I'm sorry, I didn't think anyone would be upset. I meant it as a joke."

This incident led me to ask the HR department to plan another new-manager orientation session on sexual harassment. I continue to find, these many years later, that there are myths and misconceptions about the laws regarding sexual harassment. I believe the leader not only should engage the formal training process at least once a year but also should openly address sexual harassment as a moral and power issue of great concern in the servant leader workplace.

CHAPTER NINE

Legal Issues

LET'S BEGIN WITH SEXUAL harassment because it quickly becomes a legal issue. Harassment directed at a person, rather than the environment, is a much more intense matter requiring immediate response. I've cut short and returned from business trips in order to address a harassment situation. It's important to demonstrate to the woman that the complaint is being taken seriously and something is being done. Understand that the harassment does not have to be an overt sexual proposition; it only has to be directed specifically at the person. Here, from my files, are some actual comments that led to sexual harassment complaints:

"I bet you look great in a bikini."

"Just out of curiosity, what is your bra size?"

"Did you and your boyfriend stay in the same room on your trip to Mexico?"

"What's your favorite sexual position?"

"Do you have any nude pictures of yourself?"

Yes, there was a time when those sorts of comments might have been thought of as boys just being boys, even though the comments are clearly insulting and clearly identify the woman as a sex object. Those days, thankfully, are over, but the comments have not stopped.

When a complaint of direct sexual harassment is made, you have no choice but to respond rapidly and to take the steps prescribed by your organization. These likely will include a meeting with the person against whom the complaint was made, during which he is told of the complaint and is told not only to stop the harassment but also not to even speak with the woman about it. This is a critical point. There is to be no conversation about the complaint between the woman making the complaint and the man. Furthermore, the man is not to take any action that might be interpreted as retribution, including complaining about the woman to other employees. If the man can't agree to this or if he violates it, he should be put on leave of absence until the official investigation (by the HR department or legal department) is complete.

There is no requirement that the man be fired for a first complaint as long as the company can demonstrate that it has responded appropriately to stop the harassment. However, I would make it a practice to fire any man who even implied that sexual favors would result in a promotion, a raise, or a better working situation, and I would refer to the legal authorities any man who threatened to fire a woman unless she became a sex partner.

In less serious, first-complaint cases, part of the response is for the man to be put in a position not unlike probation. A repeat offense is another matter altogether. You would think that a man who'd been through the first complaint and was operating in a de facto probationary status would cool it, but you may be surprised. I was. I close this subject by reporting that I had to fire four men, one of them a good friend, for sexual harassment. There was such pain for everyone, including the woman who complained, the men and their families, and the fellow employees, as well as for me and other leaders. Sad and foolish.

Lawsuits

You will be sued. The only question is when. Most of the time, this is a matter for the lawyers, but there is an attitude the servant leader should cultivate, and there are occasionally actions to take.

Begin with attitude: You should not consider a lawsuit a war. I think lawyers get a bad rap because, in their vigorous advocacy, they seem to be fighting. In my experience, that's not often the case. Attorneys are able to advocate fiercely in their legal roles and are still able to maintain civil relationships with their adversaries. I wish more business competitors could behave as well.

As a servant leader, you should maintain the perspective that legal actions, even ones that seem frivolous or unfair, are part of the great process of democracy. It's not that you can't become passionate, perhaps even angry, but you can't become obsessed with the plaintiff as enemy, and you can't think of the process as a war despite what you see on TV.

> Begin with attitude: You should not consider a lawsuit a war.

My group was sued a few years ago for unlawful termination. I was a witness for the defense, of course, since I was president of the group. I also had worked with the plaintiff for many years. Outside the courtroom, waiting to be called, I found myself with another employee, a woman who was a witness for the plaintiff. It was an uncomfortable moment.

Finally, I said, "Listen, we've worked together for years. I disagree with the suit. I think we were right in this matter. Regardless, the fact is someone is going to win this thing and someone is going to lose. I want you to know that you are in no jeopardy because you're testifying for Bill. When this is over, I hope we'll keep on working together just as we have."

I thought she was going to cry. I'm not sure we ever quite felt the same about one another again, perhaps a bit of residual discomfort, but we worked together productively for several more years.

Self-righteousness gives us a lot of comfort, someplace to hide our anger, a way to feel that justice is on our side. The servant leader does not fall into that trap but steps back and analyzes every situation for what it is and for what he or she can do about it.

I once worked for an editor who taught me a thing or two about humility and civility in dealing with legal situations. Our magazine, in keeping with its editorial style, published a photograph of a beautiful piece of appliqued tapestry; in addition, we offered a pattern so our readers could duplicate the project for themselves.

Unfortunately, through an administrative slipup, we did not have permission from the artist to sell a pattern. Not only that, but the artist felt that selling a pattern was a violation of her creative property and that it made her work seem less like art and more like a crafts project. She was deeply offended.

The way we first heard about her displeasure was through her lawyer, who wrote a letter threatening suit if we did not immediately withdraw the magazine from the newsstands. This would have been impossible. We did what we could, which was to stop filling the orders, return the readers' money, and send a letter of apology to them.

Our attorneys were beside themselves because the amount of damages we might be required to pay would be directly related to the extent of the exposure. This meant that every magazine sold increased the exposure, thus the potential damages.

There truly seemed no legal way out of this mess, short of a lawsuit or a costly settlement. At the time I was managing editor, so I was in the middle of it. I went into the editor's office with a list of possible actions we could take. He looked them over, then buzzed his secretary. "Liz, please get me Miss Jeffreys' telephone number." Miss Jeffreys was the designer. I was aghast.

He dialed the number.

"Miss Jeffreys? . . . Miss Jeffreys, this is Don Donaldson. We have a letter from your lawyer about our mistake in selling plans for your beautiful work of art."

Pause.

"I just want to say, Miss Jeffreys, that I can't tell you how much I regret this mistake. We just did not pay enough attention to what we were doing, and I'm as sorry as I can be. I'm willing to do anything I can to make you feel better about this and to make it up to you, but what your lawyer is asking is just not possible."

It turned out that she didn't know what the lawyer was asking and when it was explained, she agreed it was impossible.

"What would you like us to do, Miss Jeffreys?"

What she wanted was for us to stop selling the patterns. We'd already done that. And she wanted an apology and a retraction in the next issue. We'd already planned to do that and were only waiting for legal approval. In addition, the editor told her, we would send all the money we'd collected for the patterns to her and we'd destroy the patterns.

She refused the money, saying it was a matter of principle, not money, at which point the editor said,

"Well, then, Miss Jeffreys, if you'll name a charity, we'll contribute it in your name."

That was that. The matter was settled. Furthermore, Miss Jeffreys was very grateful for how she'd been treated. She told the editor that she had never wanted to sue, she just didn't want her art to be denigrated.

Our lawyers, of course, were very agitated, and said my boss had put the company at greater risk by making the call. I've never quite figured out why that might be, but it didn't matter anyway.

Am I suggesting that you take matters into your own hands? Certainly you would not be able to do something like this most of the time. I am saying that you can use your own judgment when you are about to be sued. If a personal contact has promise, then take the chance; you'll rarely be faulted by a judge for trying to settle something without going to court as long as you don't try to threaten or coerce, which as a servant leader you'd never do anyway.

In summary, you as a servant leader will not be spared the harsh realities of organizational life; they go with the territory. But if you can stay the course, maintain your balance, remain centered and focused, and act with integrity and authenticity, you can continue to create a vibrant and creative community of work while navigating the inevitable rough spots. At the same time, you will be a resource of comfort and support in some of the most troubling and challenging situations your employees face.

PART FOUR

Finding the Balance

THE DISTINGUISHED PROFESSOR AND author Peter Vaill has referred to management as "a performing art." I agree, and if we include the circus among the performing arts, then management is also sometimes a great balancing act.

The manager is always on a tightrope. The business school textbooks list "representation" as one of the characteristics of management. This means that you must represent the viewpoints, philosophies, and directives of the organization or of senior management to your people, and you must represent the concerns, interests, and ideas of your people to senior management.

What the textbooks don't tell you is that neither of those groups ever thinks you do it well enough. Senior management is likely to feel that you coddle your people, that you make excuses for them, and so on, while your people are likely to feel that you don't watch out for them enough or that they inherit a disproportionate share of the workload.

The tightrope goes with the territory; in fact, it is part of the territory. Even the most enlightened servant leaders will find themselves there from time to time, despite all efforts at open and honest communications with everyone.

But the balancing act has broader and even more important aspects than the tightrope between management and employees. For instance, there is now a broadly perceived crisis of loyalty in the American workplace. In such a setting, how does the servant leader inspire and motivate people to be their best selves and do their best work in accomplishing the mission that fulfills the purpose of the organization and the people themselves?

It is in the nature of a human enterprise that there will be disagreement and, often, conflict. This may be between coworkers, between departments or groups, and even between the leader and other leaders. What should the servant leader's response be? Even if conflict can't be resolved, how can it be managed in a way that keeps it from disrupting the mission of the individual people or the group?

And what about family and community life today? There seems to be no debate about the preoccupation with work bordering on work addiction among some groups and in some industries. It's easy to blame all this on the demands of employers, but there's more to it than that. There is plenty of evidence that some people actually prefer being at work to being at home. They report feeling more in control or less distracted. They say they are more fulfilled by their work than by family responsibilities and activities.

This becomes expressed also as an unwillingness to participate in community activities, in what might be called the responsibilities of citizenship. While some managers may not be disturbed by this and may even feel that they benefit by an employee's desire to spend more time at work than anywhere else, the servant leader should not share this shortsighted view. But what should the response be? And what, if any, responsibility should the leader feel toward the employees' personal and family well-being?

Finally, how does the leader maintain the balance in the face of crisis and even failure?

The four chapters in this section attempt to answer these questions and to provide ways to respond to the dilemmas facing servant leaders as they balance the good of the organization with the good of the people.

CHAPTER TEN

Servant Leadership and the Crisis of Loyalty

HERE'S THE CONUNDRUM: AS more and more of our businesses become driven by knowledge, information, and service, thus absolutely dependent on people for success, more and more young people think of themselves as free agents of their own careers and want to be less dependent on an organization for their sense of success.

Many executives are worried, for good reason, about what happens to loyalty in this scenario of the new workplace and the new worker. There always has been a certain social foundation in functioning organizations, an understanding between employee and company that works like an adhesive to hold the enterprise together.

Existing beyond the standard motivators of compensation and benefits, this foundation has had at its core a characteristic that, for lack of a better word, is called "loyalty." Thus the concept of a free agent, of an employee signing on to just perform the job function while building skills and experience long enough to enhance the résumé and move to the next opportunity, seems to undermine the very definition of "loyalty." If so, what happens to organizational life as we have come to know it?

My response begins with the assertion that loyalty as it was traditionally defined in so many companies was not very important anyway, but loyalty as it should be defined continues to be critical to the community of work.

Let's list some old myths about loyalty:

Myth: Loyalty should be a condition of employment.

Myth: Loyalty is only a feeling, thus is difficult to perceive with certainty.

Myth: Long hours are a sign of loyalty, the most loyal employees being those who spend the most time at the workplace.

Myth: The most loyal people are those who do not make waves but accept policies, procedures, and decisions without question or debate.

Myth: The loyal person does not seek or consider job opportunities in other organizations.

Myth: Loyalty is long-term or not at all, and can never be episodic.

These statements about loyalty probably never were accurate, and they certainly will never define loyalty in the new workplace and with the new workers. If indeed there is a "crisis of loyalty" as many observers believe, there is a persuasive argument that businesses brought it on themselves by the astonishing lack of loyalty shown to their employees during the eighties and nineties when corporations who, in the name of reengineering and efficiency and often just to impress the financial analysts, downsized thousands of workers.

The servant leader does not operate out of ego and does not expect the old-time personal loyalty to the boss. Instead, the servant leader must understand the true nature of loyalty, then work to nurture it.

Prior to all this disruption, loyalty from many of the old-paradigm executives' point of view was always one way: The employees were to be loyal to the organization. I recall in the late eighties, in the midst of so many layoffs and downsizings, a CEO once asked me, "Jim, whatever happened to good old-fashioned loyal employees?" It was all I could do to restrain myself from saying, "Well, what do you think happened? You laid them off."

Too often, loyalty was expected as a personal matter: "My people are loyal to me." And woe to the employee who talked about "our" department to someone in another department. But that was phony loyalty and was never very important to anything but the boss's ego.

The servant leader does not operate out of ego and does not expect the old-time personal loyalty to the boss. Instead, the servant leader must understand the true nature of loyalty, then work to nurture it. Start by dispelling the old myths with some facts about loyalty.

First things first: Loyalty begets loyalty.

Loyalty is not just a feeling that can't be perceived; it is a behavior or a series of behaviors. Loyalty is like love. The person who claims loyalty then does not exhibit loyal behavior is not loyal, just as the person who claims to love then does not behave accordingly does not love.

What is loyal behavior? For the employee, it is simply doing the job that is agreed upon and doing it to the best of one's ability with honesty and integrity. It is being sensitive to, and acting in, the best interest of the organization, colleagues, and peers. This is the kind of behavior that will inspire loyalty from fellow workers as well as from the organization.

For the organization and its leaders, loyalty to employees means being honest and trusting, treating people as individuals and not as numbers, responding appropriately to special needs, providing resources, and, most important, acting with integrity. That means being open in communication, sharing information, doing what you say you are going to do. This is the kind of behavior that inspires—and deserves—loyalty from the people.

MYTHS ABOUT LOYALTY

Myth: Loyalty should be a condition of employment.

Myth: Loyalty is only a feeling, thus is difficult to perceive with certainty.

Myth: Long hours are a sign of loyalty, the most loyal employees being those who spend the most time at the workplace.

Myth: The most loyal people are those who do not make waves but accept policies, procedures, and decisions without question or debate.

Myth: The loyal person does not seek or consider job opportunities in other organizations.

Myth: Loyalty is long-term or not at all, and can never be episodic.

Loyalty is not influenced by power, thus it cannot be compelled; it must be earned and deserved. Loyalty should go both ways. In fact, it should go several ways at once: company to employee, employee to company, employee to colleague, and so on. This kind of loyalty is not obsolete in the new workplace and among the new workers, and I have witnessed it in several different kinds of companies. But understand that unlike yesteryear, loyalty does not imply a lifelong commitment from either the company or the employees. Loyalty as a personal trait should most assuredly be enduring, but loyalty as behavior to fulfill a commitment can be episodic. This is a very important understanding in leading the new workers.

> *For the organization and its leaders, loyalty to employees means being honest and trusting, treating people as individuals and not as numbers, responding appropriately to special needs, providing resources, and, most important, acting with integrity.*

It is altogether possible for a person to feel and exhibit loyalty to the organization, to colleagues and peers, and to the project or product itself even for only a limited period of time. The intensity of the loyalty does not have to correlate with the tenure of the employee. In understanding this, the servant leader abandons old preconceptions about loyalty and works to create the conditions in which loyalty flourishes around whatever is being done now, today, this minute. This means accepting, without prejudice, the possibility that an employee may be loyal to the people, the place, and the job at hand, and still resign for another job a month from now.

Loyalty in the community of work has both personal and professional aspects: There must be a balance between the loyalty to one's peers and team members, one's colleagues, one's manager, and one's employees, and the loyalty extended to the community itself, including the organization and its vision.

Without these multifaceted aspects, loyalty can become distorted. I once watched a colleague defend the substandard work of another colleague, even though he knew the work was not good and would have to be redone at some point. When I asked why, he said, "I'm doing it out of loyalty to my friend." But this violated a greater loyalty to the values of the community. If loyalty requires dishonesty or the violation of trust, it is not true loyalty in the context of the workplace.

What about loyalty and layoffs? On the one hand, you as the servant leader must exemplify loyalty by exhibiting at all times the multifaceted loyalty just described. But how does it work when you have to do the difficult things such as fire or lay off an employee? How in the world does that fit with loyalty?

I've often said that if you can't say, "I love you, you're fired," then you shouldn't be in management. That may be overstated for effect, but the point is important: You must be able to feel and exhibit affection and goodwill and, yes, loyalty toward the people you have to appraise negatively or even fire. The only way to do this is by putting these sometimes drastic actions in context with your loyalty to the organization and its values. As a leader, there is no way to escape the responsibility for walking that delicate line and making those delicate judgments between the rights of the group versus the rights of the individual. There comes a time when a greater moral good is served, a greater loyalty is exhibited, by taking an action that may on the surface seem less than moral or less than loyal. This is the difficult stuff of leadership, and perhaps the defining difference between a "manager" and a "leader" is in the way that person expresses an affection and a regard for the human dignity of a person being fired.

One more point about firings and layoffs: You must recognize both the peril and the opportunity in these unfortunate actions. By the way you treat the laid-off or fired employee, you can either enhance or seriously damage the loyalty of the remaining employees.

Not long ago, I advised a CEO client that he just had to shut down a money-losing operation. It was a venture very close to his heart, but either the timing or the market or something else wasn't right. Whatever the reason, I could see no way for it to become profitable and contribute an appropriate return on the investment. Furthermore, all the money being made by the other operations was just draining away into this venture and putting the rest of the company in jeopardy.

"This is going to cost you the company if you don't act pretty soon," I told him.

He was not happy, but I pressed him. "You're paying me to tell you the truth and sometimes the truth is hard."

"But all the people . . ." he began.

"I know how you feel," I said. And I did. I had become close to this group of energetic, hardworking, young people, who, through no fault of their own, just could not make this project work. I was as distressed as anyone by the prospect of putting them on the street. I also knew that a layoff of this magnitude had the potential for devastating the morale of the remaining employees, who, out of loyalty to their friends and colleagues, might feel that the company had betrayed them and might also feel that they would be next. Many company executives failed to recognize this risk during the downsizings of the eighties and nineties, then couldn't seem to understand why morale and productivity dropped, not to mention employee loyalty.

During that time, I interviewed a group of employees who had been kept in the job after many of their friends and coworkers had been laid off. The answer was commonsense simple: The remaining employees were so traumatized that they put a lot of worry time into wondering when the next shoe would fall. They were given little or no information about the layoffs or the condition of the company, so they understandably concluded that their jobs also might be in jeopardy. This fear was exacerbated by their feeling that their laid-off coworkers had been shoddily treated.

I was straightforward with my client about this risk. "What can we do?" he asked.

We agreed to think about it and come up with a plan. Here's what we did: First, there were to be no surprises or secrets. The people who were to be laid off would be told directly and would be told first. Then the other people would be told. In those companywide meetings, the CEO sincerely demonstrated his authenticity and vulnerability by apologizing for what he had to do, then he demonstrated his sincerity and goodwill by establishing a program to support the laid-off workers.

The company promised to give first choice on any open jobs to the laid-off employees. Further, the company HR people took on an outplacement role by contacting companies in the surrounding area and other companies in the industry in the attempt to find jobs.

Next, the CEO hosted a special social event in which he recognized the achievements of the laid-off group and honored the quality of their work. This took away the possibility that he would seem to be blaming the employees for the failure of the project.

And finally, the company set aside several hundred thousand dollars for interest-free loans to the laid-off employees. The loans could be to bridge a mortgage payment or car payment, to pay for tuition, or whatever the ex-employee felt was needed. And the loans could be repaid on whatever schedule worked for the person.

When I tell this story now to groups of businesspeople, somebody will inevitably comment that "this seems like a very expensive proposition and risky as well."

But here's the result. Very few people even took advantage of the loan fund, and of those who did, no one failed to pay it back.

Furthermore, and this is the important part, the positive impact on the morale of the remaining employees was palpable. I did some focus groups in which people said things like, "I know the company did everything it could to help our friends, and I know if I ever have to be laid off, the company will help me make another start." And these are all young people, "the new workers," and the company is very technologically driven and exemplifies "the new workplace."

This dramatic demonstration of loyalty as action, loyalty being earned, and loyalty going both. ways proves to me that people, whoever they are, whatever their age, whatever their orientation to their careers, still respond to the basic humanity of servant leadership.

So engage and practice that basic humanity as a servant leader, and loyalty will take care of itself, whether in an old or a new workplace, or among old or new workers.

CHAPTER ELEVEN

Conflict

ALWAYS REMAIN MINDFUL OF the truth that most conflict in the workplace is about personality and style and not about product or process. This is not to say that most disagreement in the workplace is about style and personality. Although disagreement can turn into conflict, constructive disagreement is often the fertile medium in which better ideas grow.

The problem is that it's not always easy to discern the difference between personal conflict and disagreement, between arguments based on personal animosity and those based on professional judgment. Rarely will someone say, "I don't like working with that stupid jerk Ray, and I'm not going to agree with anything he says." More likely you'll hear something like this: "Certainly Ray's idea has some merit, but basically I think it misses the mark by quite a wide margin and doesn't get at the problem we're trying to solve. I suggest that . . . ."

There is nothing more disruptive to the work environment, to teamwork, or to morale generally than unresolved conflict. Left unaddressed, conflict will poison the atmosphere well beyond just the workers most directly involved. The question is, how do you deal with it in a way that is not judgmental but is in keeping with the best values of a caring and supportive workplace?

> *Left unaddressed, conflict will poison the atmosphere well beyond just the workers most directly involved.*

Servant leaders must realize that they cannot make people like one another. That's not even the point. Once people leave the workplace, they may not even want to speak to one another. So be it. The goal of the servant leader workplace is that people care about one another in the context of what they do together, because in that context they are mutually interdependent whether they personally like one another or not. Their connection as participants in the community of work must transcend their personal differences. Easier said than done, but this is how the servant leader must think about the issues of personal relationships, conflict, and disagreement.

Some of my Air Force experience provides helpful perspective here. I flew jet fighters for over four years, serving three of those years in France during the cold war days of the late fifties.

You might think that in a fighter squadron, so often celebrated in the popular media as a scene of constant camaraderie and friendship, there would be no personal conflict. Not true. In those days—and my experience is limited to the time before women served in the military as pilots—the equipment room was intense with testosterone. You probably would be surprised at the frequent level of fervent disagreement, conflict, and even hostility. Some of the pilots could hardly stand to spend time together. Underneath that, however, was something else, a connection far more powerful than the conflict, a connection based on mission and purpose and on the very real possibility of death and the responsibility to protect one another.

No matter how much conflict there might be, when four pilots taxied their planes to the runway, ready to leap off as a flight of four into bad weather at night, their lives utterly dependent on one another's skills and abilities, I assure you that no one was thinking about likes and dislikes, hostilities, and conflicts. No one cared about skin color, ethnicity, religion, sexual orientation, or anything else beyond flying ability and accomplishing the mission together. I now think of those flights as metaphors for how people in the workplace can care about one another in the context of the work they do together, even if they don't like one another.

The challenge for the servant leader is to try to prevent disagreement about ideas or process or product from degenerating into personal conflict. If conflict does exist, the first goal is to resolve it. If resolution doesn't seem possible, then the goal is to manage the conflict so that it does not intrude into the flow of the work and the workplace.

Preventing Conflict

The best way to keep disagreement from turning into conflict is to recognize when it's likely to happen and intervene in a positive way. An accomplished practitioner of the positive intervention is Peter Roy, former president of Whole Foods, Inc. Peter's tenure was an outstanding time of rapid growth through expansion and acquisition. If anything, the stress of success is more intense than the stress of failure, so during these heady times at Whole Foods, Peter was sensitive to the possibilities for conflict.

He told me that he adapted a simple technique called "affirmations" as a positive way of ending a meeting that had been contentious and that held the possibility of later conflict. Peter explained that, before adjourning the meeting, he would ask his executives to go around the room and "affirm" one another.

Here's how it works: Each person, in order starting wherever you wish, is affirmed by every other person present. This can be difficult, particularly when you are called upon to affirm someone with whom you've just been disagreeing vigorously. But it's effective. Peter puts it this way: "If you and I have been going at it strongly, almost in conflict, and then I have to look at you and say, 'Jim, I want to affirm that you're a smart and effective manager, a person with good ideas, and a person I can learn—and have learned—from, and that you're essentially a decent and moral person even though I may disagree strongly with you from time to time,' then that takes all the heat out of the room and allows people to return to the values that brought them together in the first place."

Yes, you'll have people who will scoff at such an idea, who will consider it too "new age," a waste of time, who would rather be in conflict than face the difficult task of civility and collegiality. But in the long run, this little exercise will contribute immensely to morale and productivity and will prevent who knows how much destructive conflict.

Affirmations can work in departments or teams, among the management group, with veteran employees or beginners. You might have to adjust the vocabulary, but the idea should remain the same. Once, in working with a group of production people, all men, it was clear that one of them—let's call him Burt—was not very well liked. Furthermore, it was clear that he didn't try to be liked and, by his attitude and behavior, may even have invited the negative feelings. So, nervously I admit, I decided to try affirmations, using a different vocabulary.

I said, "I want to try a little exercise with you guys. Could even be fun. Here's what we're going to do. We're going to choose someone and then pick on him. Only instead of saying critical stuff, we're going to compliment him."

There was a little laughter. "Are you willing?" I asked. No one jumped in with an enthusiastic yes, but there was nodding of heads, smiling, shrugging, all the usual body language of general agreement. So I continued.

"Let's begin with Burt. Now, Burt, all you have to do is sit there, and each guy here is going to tell you something he likes about you. We'll start with John. Okay, John, let Burt have the best compliments you can hit him with. Tell him what you like about him."

After the initial shock and some nervous laughter, the process began. It was like a little miracle. After a few compliments, there began to be wholehearted laughter and joking remarks such as, "Yeah, right," and "Are we talking about Burt?" Burt himself went from flabbergasted to genuinely embarrassed by the attention. We continued around the room, with everyone participating. I felt it particularly poignant when Burt paid each man a compliment.

And the effect lasted. I don't pretend to be able to explain these things, and I'm no psychologist, but I think Burt became more likeable because he felt liked, and the other men in turn felt that if he could pay them a compliment, he probably was not all that bad a guy. In retrospect, that little thirty-minute episode effected a remarkable turnaround in the interpersonal relationships of that department.

Another broader idea for conflict prevention is a technique I call the "circles of silence." This exercise, which I have introduced into several settings and which has even become institutionalized throughout one company, can become one of the defining cultural characteristics of the servant leader workplace.

It begins with the understanding that, even with the people we love most in the world, 90 percent of our conversation is about budget, planning, operations, and logistics. Think about it. Among parents, it might go like this: "Listen, you pick up Caitlin at gymnastics class, I'll get Matt at Little League, then I'll meet you here. We'll drop them off, then I'll pick up the groceries for the dinner party Saturday while you feed the kids." And the response might be, "Okay, and on your way from the store, stop by the wine shop and get a good bottle of red." And so on. Budget, planning, operations, and logistics.

But if those relationships are to remain strong, we know we have to take some time, perhaps 10 percent, to say how we feel. We have to get away from that other stuff and hang out, take a vacation, or just talk. It may not always be pleasant, but for the sake of the relationship, we are committed to creating unstructured time for these conversations.

In organizational life, it's all about budgets, planning, operations, and logistics. One hundred percent. Do we say how we feel? Of course, but the setting may be at the watercooler or over a cup of coffee or lunch or a drink after work—and it usually comes out as simple griping. It is shared among a limited number of people and never makes its way into the mainstream of daily concourse except as rumor and malcontentment.

The circles of silence change all that. This is a simple idea but difficult to effect because it requires four conditions: (1) an absolute commitment to the process by senior management; (2) the creation of a safe place in which nothing said can provoke retribution or be held against the person making the statement; (3) agreement to try the circles once a month for at least three months; and (4) time in each session, usually four hours, to let the process work.

Also, I suggest limiting the size of each group to between thirty and forty, maximum. There is no need to bring in an outside facilitator like me; anyone can do this, although you as the manager/leader should not be the facilitator. Ask for a volunteer. After the introduction, there's little to do.

In introducing the exercise, I usually say something like this: "We're going to have a meeting—yes, another meeting—but this one is different. First, there will be no chairperson. Second, there will be no agenda. We will sit in a circle in chairs. No desks. No writing materials. Then comes the hard part. For the first twenty minutes, we'll sit in silence."

You can imagine the reaction I get from people who spend their days at work in a constant state of activity. In doing. And here I'm asking them to sit silently for

FOUR CONDITIONS FOR THE
CIRCLES OF SILENCE

An absolute commitment to the process by senior management

The creation of a safe place in which nothing said can provoke retribution or be held against the person making the statement

Agreement to try the circles once a month for at least three months

Time in each session, usually four hours, to let the process work

twenty minutes. This, of course, is also doing something, but they don't think of it that way.

I tell them, "You can nap if you wish, meditate, or pray. You can roll your eyes at one another about this silly new age stuff, you can pick your fingernails and sigh deeply. But you can't speak and you can't leave the room."

Usually there is good humor about all this, although it's not unusual for people to complain that it seems like a waste of good time.

I continue, "Furthermore, after the twenty minutes have passed, you may speak only if you feel moved to

179

speak. If you don't feel moved to speak, don't speak. If you do feel moved to speak, say only how you feel. About your life, about your job, about anything. But don't say what you think or what you're going to do, and don't ask questions. Just say how you feel. Another thing, don't give other people advice. If someone has said how he feels, don't say, 'Oh, I know what you can do about that.' Instead, if you're moved to speak, say how you feel about a similar situation or about that specific situation."

I go so far as to tell them that no statement should begin with "I think" or "I want" or "I'm going to." Only, "I feel."

The beginning silence is important to the process. It not only is generally calming but also requires self-discipline on the part of the participants. Most of them will realize in a few minutes that there's nothing to do but make the best of the situation; this, in itself, is a step in the right direction. Next, most will move into some kind of meditative or reflective mood just as a result of sitting quietly. When this happens to us, our brain waves shift into another pattern that allows for a different level of communication. Nothing conscious about this; it just happens.

I don't tell them when the twenty minutes is up. Even when they've figured out that the time is up, there is a great reluctance to speak. This is quite normal and not a bad sign. If you try this in your organization, be warned that some of the participants may be negative, even hostile, to the whole idea and may say something like, "I feel this is a bunch of new age crap and a waste of time." That's normal also.

If no one speaks or if people aren't expressing their feelings, I usually break the group into smaller groups, to reduce the circle of fear. I admonish them not to talk while changing configurations. Then I try various exercises to get them talking. Here are some ideas:

"Take one minute and tell everyone in your group about something you've always wanted to do in your life but never had the chance, and how you think that would make you feel."

"Take one minute and tell everyone in your group one thing about your job that you really love."

"Take one minute and tell everyone in your group one thing about your job that you really hate."

After a couple of these, I will reconvene the whole group. What I hope is that the small group exercises have helped people relax into the process. If not, I break into small groups again, only this time perhaps twice as large as before. There are several possible exercises, but here are two that I usually save for last:

"Take one minute and tell everyone in your group about the thing in your life that gives you the most joy."

"Take one minute and tell everyone in your group about the thing in your life that gives you the most pain."

I've done this exercise well over a hundred times, and I've yet to work with a group that did not have a breakthrough of some sort, something that would open them up to the process and get them talking about how they feel.

It can become very emotional and sometimes painful. But it is always honest.

This is not group therapy and it's not twelve-step work, though there are aspects of both in the exercise. This is community building.

What, you may ask, does this have to do with organizational life, with purpose and mission, with getting the job done? Only this: What people come to realize as a result of this exercise is that, no matter what our differences may seem to be, underneath it all we are more similar than dissimilar. We love, we experience joy, we suffer pain and grief. Saying how we feel communicates a deeper understanding of who we are.

In my work with organizations, I've observed that once people connect on that level, they are more able to put their disagreements into perspective. They realize that the normal disagreements in the workplace are not about character, they're not about good versus evil, they're not about right and wrong. They are simply disagreements about what we do, not about who we are. This realization goes a long way in preventing conflict, and when conflict does arise, the circles provide an open and safe forum for putting those feelings on the table.

An executive in one of my client companies a few years ago told me that all the watercooler bitching had about disappeared as a result of the circles of silence. He said that when someone had a complaint, a colleague or coworker was likely to say, "Why don't you talk about it in the circle?"

One more thing: Once you've inculcated the circles into your organization and they've become part of your social architecture, people will not want to give them up. While you may begin with monthly meetings, there is no requirement for monthly or even quarterly circles, and eventually your organization will get to the point of convening a circle only when the need is felt and communicated, which is as it should be.

A final thought about conflict prevention. Nothing substitutes for your own awareness and readiness to respond. When you sense conflict developing between people or groups, intervene quickly with a conversation or a meeting of the parties.

Resolving Conflict

I had a boss years ago who had his own way of resolving conflict. He'd call the people into his office and say, "Okay, you two work out your damned differences and get back to work or I'll fire both of you." I admit that, while it is not the way of servant leadership, it was effective in the short run.

The problem was that what the people usually did, out of fear of losing their jobs, was to choke back their disagreements, their anger, and their hostility in a way that was not healthy for their bodies or their spirits. Inevitably, choked-back conflict manifests itself in some negative way, usually one that has a disruptive impact on the workplace. It's just a matter of time.

As a servant leader, you must be sure to ascertain the nature of the conflict. Is it an inexplicable personality conflict, a turf battle, an honest difference of viewpoint that has escalated into bad feelings, or an unhealthy competition for recognition and reward? There may be different ways to handle these, depending on your own role in the conflict.

First, fix organizational problems. Ask yourself these questions: What have I done to create or exacerbate this situation? Is this an organizational matter of someone being in the wrong job, or a structural matter of two jobs inappropriately positioned in the organization? What can I do to alleviate the situation organizationally or structurally? Often, managers, out of the archaic and misguided concept of putting people in competitive situations and letting them duke it out to see who gets the next promotion, have created impossible relationships between their people.

Even if you have not purposely created competitive situations, they still may exist. They even may be created by the perceptions of the employees themselves. Remember that we are conditioned by society to compete; the idea of competition so permeates our everyday lives that it's only natural to see ourselves in competition at work, even if that perception is not accurate. In today's workplace of increasing emphasis on teams and teamwork, on self-management, peer review, and so on, it is highly counterproductive for people to waste energy in phantom competition.

If you find you can do something structurally or organizationally to help solve or alleviate the problem, first tell the people involved what you plan to do, explain how it will help, get their reaction, ask for their cooperation, then do it.

Understand that this may not make the people happy immediately, but the objective is to correct the point of conflict, and then to address the morale issues. Don't forget that there's already conflict and there are already morale problems; you likely won't make matters worse and will create a much greater opportunity to make them better.

Once you're satisfied the structure is not at fault or has been fixed, you as servant leader can assume one of two roles in resolving conflict: the passive mediator or the directive provocateur. But always remember this: In whatever role you choose, you cannot resolve conflict between people; only they can do that. What you can do is help show them the way.

Conflicts of Viewpoint

The conflicts that usually can be resolved are based on a difference of viewpoint. These can be very legitimate differences because we are shaped by the lens through which we view the world. Men and women often see things differently; people of different racial or ethnic groups frequently have different perspectives; people of different disciplines may have very different ideas about an organizational situation. It is important that these conflicts of viewpoint not be allowed to become personal conflicts.

I was involved as a consultant to a company in which the CFO was a woman who had been promoted up through various financial jobs in the organization. She was bright, competent, and personable. Nonetheless, it was not long before she was in considerable disagreement, then conflict, with the senior vice president for sales, a man. This particular conflict is very common in companies, and this one was on the verge of becoming personal.

At the risk of oversimplifying, it was not so much a matter of gender difference as it was one born of discipline: finance versus sales. The sales vice president's viewpoint was that the revenue stream of the company depended on sales; therefore sales should be supported in all its initiatives. By "supported," he meant given resources, particularly money. He was fond of saying things like, "It takes money to make money," and, in lobbying for larger travel budgets, "You gotta see 'em to sell 'em." Using war metaphors, he felt that his salespeople were out there every day, in the line of fire, in harm's way, the first out of the trenches and into the fray, and so on. And he had a point. His people were the first contact point with the customers, so why not give them all the support they wanted? They shouldn't be nitpicked to death about every lunch and cab fare.

The CFO's viewpoint, on the other hand, was that the salespeople behaved like arrogant high schoolers and spent money like drunken sailors. They were not reliable stewards of the company's money, they played fast and loose with expense accounts, turned them in late and obviously padded them. She felt that just because the salespeople were the first contact with customers and were, she admitted, under a lot of pressure to produce revenue, they should not be coddled or allowed to operate under a different set of standards from everyone else. She liked to say things like, "Accountability is everyone's responsibility," and "If everyone else in the company spent money this way, we'd be bankrupt."

Believe me, both of these executives held reasonable viewpoints. Salespeople should be given the resources to do the job; that's where the revenue comes from. At the same time, financial stewardship is everyone's responsibility. The problem in this conflict was that both of them were right in their viewpoint but wrong in their interpretation of the situation. The salespeople were not spending money like drunken sailors; they were spending money like salespeople, but to a financial person it seemed irresponsible. The CFO was not nitpicking; she was assuring accuracy and safeguarding the company's assets the way financial people are motivated to do, but to the salespeople it seemed as if she didn't trust their honesty.

The larger problem when two executives are in conflict is that their attitudes inevitably filter into their organizations and are taken up by their people, so that sooner or later this would no longer be between the CFO and the VP of sales, but would degenerate into a general air of hostility between the financial department and the sales department.

I was asked by the CEO to help resolve this conflict. I used a simple but effective technique. I asked them to switch roles. The CFO had to assume the viewpoint and make the argument for the salespeople, and the sales VP had to assume the viewpoint and make the argument for the CFO.

At first, they objected to "this game," but I persevered, asking them to adjourn to their own offices for half an hour to develop their arguments. "It's important," I said, "that you take the role seriously because who knows, you may end up in a job like this one day. So think seriously about it."

The objective of the exercise is not to get them to change their viewpoints but to develop insight and understanding about the other's viewpoint. Then the last step is to have them work jointly on a process or procedure that will satisfy both viewpoints. I asked both the CFO and the VP separately to write a procedure that would satisfy their concerns. Then they were to get together, share their procedures, and see if the two could be turned into one. It worked.

I won't claim that this eliminated all friction for all time, but it did give them a process for addressing their differences in the future.

188

Most of these conflicts begin as simple differences of perspective or opinion. They may even become constructive disagreements from which good ideas or solutions evolve. The most important thing you can do as a servant leader is bring the people together, face-to-face, to discuss the differences and the disagreements before they reach a point of conflict or hostility. This requires that you remain aware of these processes—and there may be several at the same time in any given workplace—

> *The most important thing you can do as a servant leader is bring the people together, face-to-face, to discuss the differences and the disagreements before they reach a point of conflict or hostility.*

so that you can respond. If conflicts of viewpoint are not aired and resolved, they easily become personal.

Conflicts of Personality

Conflicts of personality are more difficult because, unlike a conflict based on the perspective of a different discipline, there often is no rational reason for the personal conflict. It's all perception and it's all emotion.

Your first decision is to decide whether you can personally intervene or whether you need someone from outside your area. One way or another, there must be an intervention. Too many managers hope these situations will resolve themselves. They won't.

If you feel particularly aligned or sympathetic with one employee in the conflict, then call in someone else for the intervention. If either employee has the perception that you have a favorite in the fight, call in someone else. Otherwise—and if at all possible—do the intervention personally.

In these situations, you should begin the process as mediator, asking questions, trying to establish a civil conversation between the participants. Here are some possible questions: "Is there anything you like about each other. If so, what is it?" (A variation on affirmations.) "If you could change the other person to your own liking, what would you do?"

If possible, you're trying to take the heat out of the situation and encourage them to recognize one another's humanity. But as I have said many times, our organizations are human enterprises and, as such, are subject to the vagaries and irrationalities of the human condition. If you can't make a conversation work, then I suggest becoming more provocative and directive.

Here's one useful technique, assuming that there are two people in conflict, which is most often the case. The technique also is effective with three people.

First, set aside at least three hours and tell the affected employees to do the same. Then pick a neutral place, preferably a room outside your department. Go to a hotel if you have to. Make sure you have three comfortable chairs, with their two chairs facing each other and yours generally to the side, in the middle and approximately at a right angle to theirs. Have water, coffee, or soft drinks in the room.

The Opening Statement

Make an opening statement in your own words. Here's what I have found effective: "We're here because there is a serious conflict between you. This conflict is distracting to other employees as well as to me, and I suspect that it is undermining your own morale. The objective of this meeting is to achieve a better understanding of the conflict, of your own roles in it, and to determine how you are going to work to overcome it. In this process, it is important that you honestly express your feelings and attitudes. I won't allow any dancing around the issues or making nice with one another because I'm in the room. In other words, you're going to have to own your stuff.

"At the outset I want to say that I value both of you as employees and as people. If that weren't the case, we wouldn't be here. I'm not here to judge; I'm here only to facilitate this conversation. I also want us to proceed with the presumption of goodwill, to proceed with the acknowledgment that this is not a war and it's not a game. There won't be any losers unless we all lose, and there won't be any winners unless we all win.

"If at any point you want to take a break, okay. But if you want to leave without some resolution, that's not okay. This may not be our last meeting, but I must affirm to you that we are going to achieve at least the first step toward an understanding before we leave today."

This may sound tough, but facilitating this conversation—as difficult as it is for everyone including you—may well be the most caring leadership you can provide for these employees. And it sometimes requires confrontation; to paraphrase William Sloane Coffin, the nationally known and respected minister, even compassion often requires confrontation.

The Technique

Regardless of your opening statement, the employees most likely will still try to "make nice" with one another, avoiding the direct conflict. Remember that they haven't been fighting in the halls or at the water fountain; they've probably been waging their battle in memos or e-mails and with fellow employees. It is important that you get them to break through the dishonest veneer of congeniality and to confront their feelings honestly.

Ask each to tell his or her story of the problem. There's no time limit on this part, and the other employee and you should listen. Sometimes the storyteller will veer off into another area or begin talking about a third person not present. Interrupt that by saying, "Let's not discuss anyone who's not here right now. If it becomes important, we'll involve that person later." It's not unusual in these circumstances for both employees to want to avoid the confrontation by scapegoating another person or another department or "the system." Don't allow it.

After the first one talks about the problem, then give the other person a turn. After that, take a turn yourself and summarize your understanding of the conflict. Try to focus on the points of professional conflict or disagreement. Remember, there's nothing you can do about how these folks feel toward one another; you're not trying to change their feelings, only their behavior, thus their performance and their impact on others.

Then give each one another turn if you feel there's more story to be told. If not, begin the next stage—the interview. Here's where you take over the conversation and ask pointed questions. Let's assume the names are Bob and Sally, that Bob is middle-aged and Sally is in her thirties. It could go like this:

"Okay, Bob, tell me exactly what Sally is doing to interfere with your ability to do your job. Then tell me what she's doing to interfere with other people's ability to do their jobs."

Then turn the tables. "Sally, respond to Bob. Tell him your perspective on that, then tell me what Bob is doing to interfere with your ability to do your job and with other people's ability to do their jobs."

This is the most difficult part of the conversation because you're trying to push them beyond their own set stories, beyond the position they've rehearsed, and into a more spontaneous response mode. Almost like a cross-examination but without hostility. Keep pushing until you feel they're dropping the masks and are being honest. Only then will you be able to get to the real issues and to some steps for solving the problem.

Sometimes you have to push pretty hard. I was involved recently in resolving conflict between two employees who were of the age and gender I just described. After they danced and danced around each other for an hour or so, I finally looked at the man and said: "Bob, isn't it true that you think Sally is a pushy, smart-aleck kid who just waltzed into this place and acts as if she's the only one who knows how to do a damned thing right? Isn't that true?"

Bob sputtered, "I never said anything like that!"

"Perhaps not," I said, "but isn't that what you really think?"

"I wouldn't put it like that," he protested.

"Well, then, use your own words and tell us how you would put it."

He was silent for several seconds, then said, "I've been around here awhile and I think I've learned a few things, but Sally acts as if nobody can teach her anything." He was visibly shaken by this admission.

I continued, "So I hear you saying that Sally doesn't respect your knowledge and experience."

But I didn't let either of them answer. Instead, I said, "It's your turn, Sally. Isn't it true that you think Bob is an old fuddy-duddy who's been around too long, who's yesterday's news, and who ought to consider early retirement?"

Sally was already shocked by the conversation; now it was her turn to be shaken. "I don't think that at all," she said.

"So why does Bob feel you don't respect him? Tell him what you do think."

She, too, was silent awhile. (I always just let the silence sit there; I never try to artificially keep the conversation going. Silence often is the most effective part of the conversation at this stage.) Finally, she said, "I don't like being treated like a kid who doesn't know anything, and I always find myself disagreeing with Bob's belief that everything has to be done a certain way."

I let that sit awhile, then said, "Now I hear you saying that Bob doesn't respect your knowledge or your ideas."

After going back and forth on this subject awhile, I asked them to tell me how they thought the conflict could be resolved. What could they do to avoid these misunderstandings about the other's perceptions? I suggested that they get together for coffee once a week and be honest with each other about how things were going between them. Then I asked them to do some affirmations (see page 174). It was as simple as saying, "Is there anything about the other person that you like? If so, say so and let's end on a good up-note." (It is often good technique in a particularly hostile situation to disarm the participants at the beginning by saying something like, "Okay, let's start this meeting with each of you saying something that you like about the other.")

Understand several things about this process: You might need several sessions. You always have to be a kind of traffic cop—stopping people from responding in the wrong places, postponing a subject till later, giving each a turn, and insisting on no interruptions, and so on. And stick with it. I have seen people in conflict go through this process and eventually become close colleagues and even friends.

Managing Conflict

If after a resolution session like the one just described, the situation seems impossible, the best you can hope for is that the conflict can be managed in a way that does not disrupt the workplace or intrude on the lives of other workers.

But here's where you have to be firm. First say to the employees, "Look, this is not about liking the other person, it's about working together in a way that doesn't keep the two of you distracted and unhappy, and in a way that doesn't distract your fellow employees. So, let's get to the operative issue here: Tell me, how do you think he [or she] does his [or her] job? Also tell me, how does what he [or she] does keep you from doing what you're supposed to do?" Ask both people to write their answers.

The next step is to make them responsible for managing their conflict. You can consider an organizational solution such as transferring one of the employees, simply separating them physically so they don't have to work together. But you may not have that option.

They must be held responsible for their behavior and for their part in assuring the continued functioning of the community of work. So ask them to prepare a plan, much like a strategic plan, with strategies they intend to employ in working peacefully and productively together. Their plan should emphasize not how they want the other person to change or what they want the other person to do, but how they plan to change and what they plan to do. This should then take the form of a written commitment and be made part of the performance standards so that they will understand that their job will be judged satisfactory only if they live up to this commitment (see performance standards, chapter 5).

You should insist that they make time once a week for coffee or lunch together; in turn, you should meet with them from time to time, to assess the situation. Your hope, of course, is that the conflict will move toward resolution.

Be prepared that this may not work, and realize that there are those situations in which, for the sake of the other employees, you may have to fire one or both of the ones in conflict. (See firing, chapter 7.) Your very best conflict resolution and management techniques just may not be good enough. Sad but true.

Managing Your Own Conflict

A final consideration about conflict resolution and management: What if you're the one in conflict?

We want to believe that as servant leaders we can prevent conflict by inculcating the characteristics described in chapter 1, and most of the time that will be true. But you will have differences of viewpoint and opinion, and you may have those differences with other managers or leaders who do not practice servant leadership and who, in fact, may be more comfortable in the old winner-loser paradigm. If so, they see differences of viewpoint in a bipolar way: You disagree with them; therefore you're the enemy who must be defeated.

The tricky part of managing conflict with these folks is in refusing to play the power games while still maintaining the validity of your viewpoint. Some of the techniques are not dissimilar from managing conflict between other people.

It begins by attempting to prevent a discussion from becoming heated. By "heated" I mean "angry." I'm not referring to a normally vigorous discussion in which viewpoints may be expressed enthusiastically and with passion. I am referring to a discussion that may degenerate into anger and personal attack.

Trust your judgment in determining when a discussion has the potential of becoming heated. This could be based on such factors as the participants, your experience in discussing controversial subjects or differing viewpoints with them, the history of your whole relationship with them, your knowledge of their relationship with others, and their style of presentation. Some people just seem to consider every meeting an invitation to a confrontation; furthermore, they seem to enjoy it. Their expectation or desire, however, does not impose upon you any obligation to do it their way.

I once had a delicate relationship with one of the senior officers in our company. He had come from another company in which, apparently, confrontation was the preferred meeting style, so he came to meetings with the attitude that there was going to be a fight. His tone was sometimes angry, sometimes dismissive and supercilious, but never conciliatory. He resorted to foul language to make his points stronger (in his view anyway), and he frequently humiliated people lower in the hierarchy.

In my first meeting with him, he slammed papers on the table, sighed deeply as if disgusted by what was being said, and even shuffled through papers and read while others were speaking. And this was supposed to be a simple informational meeting, something of a get-acquainted session. I confess I was astonished, and I confess that I was angry at his rudeness. I thought, "What an asshole." But I took a couple of deep breaths and held my peace, I refused to confront him. Instead, speaking for my staff as well as for myself, I asked one of my disarming conflict resolution questions: "John, what have we done to make you so angry?"

He was taken aback and, if anything, seemed angrier. "You haven't done anything to make me angry," he snapped. "And what makes you think I'm angry?"

"You just seem angry. In fact, John, you seem a little hostile, as if we've done something wrong."

"Listen, Jim, if I'm angry you'll know it."

Then he told me that he didn't like the format of some of my group's financial reports, that he felt we'd kept him out of the loop, and he wanted us to know that he was going to be part of this company whether we liked it or not. (I never found out what had made him feel out of the loop or not part of the company.)

To the shock of my staff people, I apologized to him. I told him that if I or any of my people had done anything to make him feel unwelcome or not part of the company, he should tell me, because that was surely not our intent. I know that, at that point, he felt he'd "won" something. He relaxed. We continued and adjourned on a fairly upbeat note, except that I knew some of my staff were still stinging from his insults.

So when I returned to my office, I phoned him. "John, I think we should have a personal talk. I didn't think it would be appropriate for the two of us, both senior officers, to get into a confrontation in front of our staff people, so I decided not to disagree with you in the meeting.

But I want you to know that I found your behavior to be not only unacceptable but also unproductive."

"That doesn't matter to me. I don't give a damn what you find unacceptable."

Once again, he saw a fight coming and was drawing his line in the sand.

"I apologize again, John. I'm not making myself clear. What I'm saying is that I don't think a meeting conducted with anger can ever be a productive meeting."

"You seem a little scared of anger."

Notice the challenging and accusatory word, "scared." This guy just couldn't seem to resist trying to pick a fight. And the weird thing was that we were not even in disagreement about any business matter, just behavior.

I didn't take the bait.

"No, John, I'm not scared of anger. But let me tell you my reaction to anger. It is certainly appropriate to express anger, but I don't think you can act effectively if you act in anger. And it strikes me that you're very comfortable acting in anger."

"That's the way I am, Jim, and you'll have to get used to it if you're going to work with me."

It was time to try another question. "So, John, if I could say something right now that would make you feel okay about this discussion, that would give you some sense of comfort that we'd had a productive conversation, what would it be? Tell me what to say and I'll say it."

He was silent. I like to think he was flabbergasted.

After what seemed a long time, he said, "We have to work together for the good of the company, and I just want to know that you'll express your views strongly and let me express mine strongly. That's how I work."

"Okay," I said, "I'll express my views strongly, very strongly in fact. But . . . ," and I emphasized the word by pausing, "I will not express my views angrily. I will not use foul language. I will not try to humiliate your staff people. I will not shuffle papers and ignore you or your staff, and I will pay attention when you or your staff people speak. Is that fair enough?"

By saying what I would not do, I was able to point out what he had done that was so offensive. He got it, but he only said, "Fair enough." I know he got it because after that, his behavior changed. I heard from other senior staff that he was the same old John in their meetings, but he was a different person with me and my staff.

Why? I don't know for sure, but I believe that under the old win-lose paradigm, some people feel threatened and under attack—even if they're not—until they can feel in control. In the phone conversation with John, my intention was twofold: One, I wanted to be sure he understood what I disapproved of in his manner and behavior; and two, I wanted to try to take away any perceived threat he might feel.

Over the next several months, John had his relapses, but generally we developed a good working relationship. In fact, after he left the company, I once saw him in New York and we had a lunch at which he told me that he'd learned a lot from me—one of the best compliments I've ever had.

If you can't prevent another person from being an angry participant in a discussion, thus cannot take the heat out of the room, then you must focus on your own behavior in the midst of the heat. You must advocate for your viewpoint without letting yourself become "the enemy" or seeing others as "the enemy." I know it's very difficult to remain calm, grounded, and centered when others around you are agitated, but this is another test of servant leadership and an important lesson to demonstrate to your people, because when they see you remaining calm in the midst of a heated discussion, they themselves are calmer, more centered, and more productive.

And while others in the old paradigm may choose to think of you as the enemy, it's important for you to do everything you can to disabuse them of that attitude. Attempt to find out why they feel that way. Try the disarming questions. Keep a dialogue going between formal meetings. What you do not want to encourage in any way is an ongoing competitive relationship in which another person is always circling you warily, ready to attack at the slightest perceived provocation. You can prevent this only through open and honest communication. I can't tell you how many businesspeople I've seen who live with hostility toward one another rather than sitting down and talking through their differences. Instead they choose—and I do mean choose because hostility and conflict are as much a choice as reconciliation and cooperation—to maintain a relationship steeped in anger. This is not only unproductive for the business, it's also unhealthy for the people.

Finally, remember that people, even you, make mistakes. Though you may evolve into the most accomplished servant leader, you still may lose your cool from time to time. You may get into one of those situations in which you see red, you just can't contain yourself, and you become angry and hostile. What then?

> *Remember that people, even you, make mistakes.*

If that happens, just get through it, and when you can, pull yourself together and apologize to anyone who has been the object of your anger. Yes, apologize. Apologize even for whatever perceived wrong or slight the other person or persons may feel.

Please abandon the old-fashioned notion that it is a sign of weakness for a manager or leader to apologize. To the contrary, it's just the opposite. By apologizing you demonstrate that you're a big enough person to know yourself and to admit mistakes, or even to take the blame for someone's perception of your wrongdoing, and to do it without fear of old definitions of "strong" or "weak." Furthermore, it signals that you recognize that you have shortcomings and that you are still willing to learn from them.

After the apology, you should then continue with the business at hand. Let's say you became angry and shouted or used inappropriate language. Your response could go like this: "Well, Janet, I lost it. I'm sorry, and I owe you an apology for using abusive language. It was inexcusable, and I ask your forgiveness." Then pause long enough to give Janet a chance to respond. Chances are she'll accept the apology, though she may want to also complain or express her feelings of hurt or anger. Just listen.

But the apology and its acceptance don't preclude the need to achieve a better understanding about the situation that made you angry. You should continue the discussion along these lines: "Thank you very much, Janet. I appreciate your understanding, and I promise to try not to let my temper get the best of me in the future. But if we can continue the discussion—and this time I'll be calm about it—I do think it's important for us to talk about this and for you to hear and understand why I was angry, just as I need to hear and understand why you did what you did."

You will have your own variations on these words, of course, but the point is to express your regret, to demonstrate your vulnerability, to be accepting of the other person's response, but to continue to move the subject toward resolution.

CHAPTER TWELVE

The Responsibilities of Family and Community Life

THERE'S A LOT OF talk about families in our society, and there's a lot of talk about community. Everyone does it—politicians, educators, church leaders, businesspeople, scholars. But much of this talk is just talk. Even family people themselves often pledge more allegiance in words to family and community than they show through their actions. In fact, if there is a discernible national trend, it is that more of today's workers are on the job for more hours than the workers of twenty years ago. Not only that, surveys indicate that a significant number of people would actually rather be at work than at home. They report feeling more in control, less hassled, better focused, and more able to feel a sense of accomplishment.

No news here, but what does this mean to the leader? Isn't a person who'd rather be at work than anywhere else a real asset? Isn't this the kind of person you want on the job? So what if employees choose to spend more time at work than at home, so what if they feel they don't have time to participate in the world outside of work?

Long Hours, Burnout, and the Job as Hiding Place

So this: If one thing is irrefutably clear, it is that a person who does not achieve a reasonable balance between work and personal time is a person who will not remain productive for very long. It seems to happen in one of two ways. First are the people who become work addicted and feel that nothing else in life matters as much as the job, so they find reasons to work, then use that as an excuse to avoid any other kind of activity. This is unhealthy for the people and the organization because burnout, a serious health problem, or a crumbling home life is the inevitable result. Next are the people who become so psychologically and emotionally overburdened by work that they can no longer find meaning in their work and thus become disillusioned. These people suffer a different kind of burnout; they're the ones who ask, "Is this all there is?" and who make ill-considered decisions to "make a change," to "try something else," only to discover that the problem was not with the job but with them.

Remember this: Burnout is not a crisis of time, it is a crisis of the spirit. If people who seem to be working hard cannot find meaning in their work, they will burn out one way or the other. There can be no problem more deserving of the leader's attention, and you should act to prevent these situations rather than wait until burnout is imminent. It's not possible, or even appropriate, for you to assure that your employees devote time and energy to their home and family, but you can assure that they have time to do so and that their jobs can't be used as hiding places.

> *Remember this: Burnout is not a crisis of time, it is a crisis of the spirit.*

Part of being present, of paying attention, is being aware of the work habits of your employees. I realize that most work has its peak periods, that we all have to put in nights and weekends from time to time, but if you have an employee doing that all the time, then you have a problem that needs attention.

First determine what the employee is actually doing. Is he or she just sort of being there without any apparent focused activity? If so, that's one kind of problem. Or is the employee actually doing productive work during all these times? If so, that's another problem.

In my group, I always made it a practice to notice when people had signed into our building on the weekends or were staying late at night. I wasn't checking on them; to the contrary, I wanted to identify anyone who seemed to be spending too much time at the workplace.

And I made sure to send clear signals that working nights and weekends was not a key to success in our group. If it had to be done at times, fine. If someone took extra time and accomplished a special project of merit, that person would be appreciated and rewarded. But all my managers knew that I considered it a negative sign if a person made a habit of working a lot of extra hours.

Soon after I first became president of the group, I recall a manager bragging to me about one of his employees. "Jerry is one of the hardest workers in the company," he said. "He's here every night, on most Saturday mornings, and sometimes on Sunday."

"And you consider that a good thing?" I asked.

"Of course," he said, "I wish all my people were like Jerry." Then sensing, I suppose, that I might question the practice, he continued, "Don't you? I mean, doesn't that say Jerry's conscientious and a hard worker?"

"I'm not questioning that," I said, "but I also know a lot of people who are conscientious and hardworking but who don't spent all that time at it. In a situation like this," I continued, "I usually find one of two questions needs answering. One is, what's wrong with Jerry? The other is, what's wrong with the job? In other words, it makes me wonder if Jerry has a problem that keeps him from accomplishing his job in the time given, or on the other hand, if the job itself is structured so that it can't be done during regular hours. If the former, we need to work with Jerry to help him become more proficient and productive. If the latter, then you need to do something about it." I paused and then said, "And no, I don't wish all our people put in the hours that Jerry does."

This was a shocker to the manager. This violated what he'd been taught about identifying "hard workers" and about equating long hours with accomplishment. If you haven't noticed, the two don't necessarily correlate.

My concern with employees spending too much time at the job may seen counterintuitive with my responsibilities to the mission and purpose of the business, but remember, as we said in chapter 2, that part of the vision of an organization is built on shared values. I felt that overwork was not, or should not be, one of the values. If we succeeded in accomplishing our mission to fulfill our purpose while also working our people to the point that their lives became unbalanced, then we would not be living our vision. And sooner or later we would not be able to accomplish our mission.

This requires that the servant leader take the long view and not fall victim to the temptation to settle for increased productivity in the short-term. I know it's done a lot, particularly by managers who want to push up the short-term results just so their record will look good enough to move to the next big opportunity. This is exactly what some of the gunslinger CEOs did during the eighties and nineties with all their downsizing and restructuring, then once they collected their stock options and moved on, the next CEO often inherited an eviscerated company and a dispirited workforce. But that's another story. Suffice to say that these guys were not servant leaders.

My point is not that I find something inherently wrong in putting in a lot of hours, but that I know the long-term key to achieving results is in maintaining a workforce of people who are balanced and happy, thus productive. I worry that people who are at the workplace too much are simply not at home and in the community enough. As I said earlier, there's really not much you can do to assure that your people spend time with their loved ones—that would be meddling where you don't belong—but you can assure that they don't use their work as an excuse for not being present to the other aspects of their lives.

Even though you will avoid intruding into employees' personal lives, you should also be aware that, as people come to realize you care about their lives outside the workplace, they may from time to time share their personal problems—sometimes even their most intimate ones. If so, listen, but don't give advice even if asked to do so. You can't be a marriage counselor or therapist. But you should consider it a good sign that the characteristics you exhibit as a servant leader have built such a level of trust and confidence in you, not only as a leader but also as a person. So what you can do, and should do, is respond with understanding and sympathy, realizing that often what is sought is simply someone to talk to.

And you can respond as an organizational leader as well, making sure the person is aware of employee assistance programs and other forms of support and, if necessary, helping the person get connected with those programs. As a normal operating practice, the servant leader always should do everything institutionally possible to support family-friendly programs such as flextime, family leave, child-care programs, and so on. Many companies these days are offering work-life arrangements that accommodate working mothers, as well as flextime and flexday programs that recognize parents' needs to attend sporting events, doctor appointments, and other obligations.

Servant leaders will welcome these arrangements, even though they may not seem "efficient." The companies offering these programs report that they are effective in building employee commitment and increasing productivity. The work-life specialist of a large midwestern farm implement manufacturer put it this way: "People in general want more out of life than just their job. They want a company to recognize them as a whole person. Workers are willing to give employers 110 percent effort on the job in return for flexibility in scheduling or other work-life benefits."

Be aware, however, that there is a shocking reaction to these programs from some managers. One of the most disturbing reports I read was about managers who stigmatize the employees who take advantage of the company's work-life benefits. In other words, the manager lets it be known that, while the company may offer such benefits, the employee who takes advantage of the benefits is not a "team player." If you are in an executive position, you should be aware of this possibility and should communicate to all your managers your disapproval of such attitudes.

> *You should also be willing to bend the rules from time to time, and you should remain open to temporary alternative working situations if the need seems compelling.*

You should also be willing to bend the rules from time to time, and you should remain open to temporary alternative working situations if the need seems compelling.

I often ask my workshop groups to respond to this situation: "Suppose you have an employee with a serious family problem, let's say a sick child, and the employee needs a special work arrangement for awhile. Do you respond, perhaps as a parent yourself, with understanding and compassion and an intention to work with the employee until the crisis passes? Or do you say, 'I feel bad about that; I'm a parent myself; but we have to get the work done around here'?"

It's a trick question, because the answer is "both." You have to respond with understanding and compassion and support, doing whatever you can to ease the workload and accommodate a different work schedule—and you have to get the work done. Once again, the servant leader is challenged to embrace a paradox.

I've always urged that leaders manage people one at a time and not in groups, and that leaders respond to people's individual human needs as the situation demands, even if that means bending the rules and making special arrangements. The objection I most often hear is that other employees will resent this special treatment, but I've found that if the leader is open and honest about what he or she is doing and makes it known that any similar situation will be treated with the same consideration, people are appreciative rather than resentful. Not only that, they will pitch in to help get the work done during this difficult period.

Of course, there may be mitigating circumstances, and it may not be possible to help in the way you wish. Even so, you should express your willingness to help and explain why you can't do it at this time. These are matters of judgment, but you should always do all you can to support your employees during times of family need. You'll find that if you remain aware and ready to respond, there will be much opportunity to demonstrate not only your belief that people should keep their lives balanced but also your willingness to support them in that endeavor. This commitment to service is a hallmark of servant leadership, and I promise that you'll be rewarded many times over, both as a person and as a leader.

Finally, all the lessons you try to teach your employees about balancing their lives and their work must be applied to yourself as well. You must model the balanced life if you expect others to work toward a balanced life. You can't jawbone the idea of personal time with home and family and community while spending endless hours at your own job.

And regardless of what you have achieved as a centered and grounded person, you are not immune to the risks concomitant with letting your life get out of balance: burnout, health problems, alienation from family and friends. So pay attention and count yourself among those to be served.

Community Involvement

The realm of community activities offers great potential for the kind of employee involvement that can have significant payoff for your organization as well as for the employee. I've always felt that some of my most important experiences came from volunteer work with community arts groups and voluntary health agencies.

Think about it for a moment: In most of these groups, you work with volunteers, people who are there because they want to be there and they want to make a difference. But sometimes there is a great gap between their noble intentions and their ability to do the job they've volunteered to do. Yet you can't fire a volunteer, so this presents a particular challenge and a unique learning experience. It becomes a valuable lesson in how to make a team work together and accomplish its goals even though some team members might be considered "weak links." Furthermore, it's a lesson in how to give those so-called weak links an opportunity to contribute in a way that makes the best use of what they can do and that honors them for it.

Encourage your employees to serve on committees and boards, to do hands-on service work, fund-raising, and so on. And give them the time off to attend the meetings and special events. All of these provide excellent opportunities for both professional and personal growth. And it goes without saying that your organization's reputation in the community will be greatly enhanced.

One of my employees some years ago began volunteering with a local group that supports activities with underprivileged children. He became so involved and committed that he emerged as a top leader of the group, was able to raise its visibility, and helped assure its long-term viability. There is still a special recognition award, named for him, that is given annually to an outstanding volunteer. And today, even though the employee is retired, the company's reputation still benefits as a result of his efforts with that community group.

One note of caution: I have known employees to become so engaged by their volunteer activities that they begin to neglect their jobs. Because the community activities are so important and often so compelling, the employees can begin to equate the volunteer work with their professional work. They also may find the volunteer work more personally rewarding or perhaps just more interesting. After all, the volunteer enjoys a great deal of freedom of action and usually gets to see direct and immediate results from the effort. Plus, it's a change of routine.

And this doesn't just affect low performers; it can impact your best people. Believe me, it's not difficult to build a rationale for taking more time to do good work in the community, but it's very difficult for you to help the employee bring it back into perspective and balance while not putting a damper on the activity or the enthusiasm for it.

The key is to always direct any discussion right back to the performance standards. If the employee is meeting the standards and achieving the results, your intervention may be a matter of expressing concern that a declining attention to the job could result in not meeting the standards. In these cases, you are not curtailing the volunteer activity, and a simple conversation may be enough to effect a change of pattern by the employee.

If the results are declining or standards are not being met, a more direct intervention is required. You may never face this problem, but if you notice it happening, move quickly to discuss it with the employee and agree on some guidelines that will refocus effort on the job while maintaining the opportunity for volunteer work.

As for yourself, community service is just a natural extension of servant leadership, which, as you evolve, will find its expression in every facet of your life. As Marian Wright Edelman says, "Service is the rent we pay for living."

I know businesspeople who like to say that a business's only responsibility is profit, and that by making a profit, the business creates jobs, pays taxes, and so on. There is certainly some truth in this point of view, but it neglects the fact that business operates in, and is part of, a complex educational, economic, social, and political ecosystem from which business derives enormous benefit. In this context, corporate citizenship is a necessity, and part of that citizenship is expressed by accommodating the community volunteer efforts of its employees. This is not a new idea; in fact, before the time of retail giants, main street businesses and businesspeople were the backbone of community activity.

Just as you must model the balanced life, as a servant leader it is important that you also model community volunteerism and involvement. If you keep your light under a bushel by expressing your leadership only in your workplace, then both you and the world will be greatly deprived.

CHAPTER THIRTEEN

Leadership When Things Go Wrong and Times Are Bad

LEADERSHIP AND MANAGEMENT ARE a lot easier when times are good, but organizational life runs in cycles, so like it or not, times are also going to be bad. This simple and irrefutable truth, particularly acute in business, reasserted itself dramatically into the public consciousness early in 2001 when our booming economy rather abruptly slowed down, accompanied by business failures, plant closings, and layoffs. For many of the executives who in their management careers had never experienced a downturn, it provoked shock and disillusionment.

An even harsher reality for some of the executives in publicly held companies was the realization that the Wall Street analysts are not very understanding about cycles; they care only about increasing earnings every quarter over the same quarter a year earlier. What this means during a downturn is that these executives often will push their operations into a crisis mode, making long-term solutions to short-term problems, solutions that will come back to haunt them when times are good again. One of my CEO heroes, experienced in the ups and downs of running a company, used to say, "If you live quarter to quarter, you'll die quarter to quarter."

This is not to make light of the very real pressure forced onto corporation executives by Wall Street, boards of directors, and stockholders, but the fact is that they are not alone. Any kind of leadership is simply much more difficult when times are so bad they require various short-term cost-cutting measures.

And I think that servant leaders fall under particularly intense pressure. It's amazing how often good leadership practices seem to come into question in times of crisis. It's as if the old-paradigm managers have just been waiting for an excuse to point the finger at servant leadership and say, "I told you so; I knew all this soft management stuff would backfire someday." And it doesn't matter how well your employees have performed or what results you've managed to achieve. History is full of examples of people who had been regarded as miracle workers, then were later crucified.

And there are many managers out there who are all too willing to sacrifice their values on the altar of crisis. I've known people I thought to be good leaders who, when tough times came, seemed to feel justified in returning to the old top-down, command-control type of management, as if saying, "When times get tough, we gotta stop making nice."

This attitude, in my opinion, is dramatic evidence of how difficult servant leadership is versus how easy the old tough guy stuff is. If there is a time when it's particularly challenging for servant leaders to stay the course, it is in the face of crisis or failure. Whereas the conventional wisdom has been that the leader must be in control, the true servant leader abandoned the control notion long ago, and realized that he or she may influence people and events but cannot control them.

This requires faith and courage; faith in the efficacy of servant leadership and courage to see it through or even to lose one's job. It's true that most senior executives or boards of directors are not comfortable with a manager/leader who does not claim to be in control, and are likely to criticize the servant leader. In addition, some employees may be more comfortable with the old ways during a crisis because it seems to offer a sense of certainty if they can feel someone is "in control."

But servant leadership is not only good-time leadership. Its value to you and your people has even more meaning and impact during the times when people are worried and struggling.

What do people need most during those times? First, they still need to be able to find meaning in their work and to feel it is important. Next, they need your honest appraisal about the real conditions of the economy, the market, and the possible impact on their jobs. And finally, they need the reassurance of seeing you, the leader, remaining calm and centered and focused in the midst of the crisis.

> *Servant leadership is not only good-time leadership. Its value to you and your people has even more meaning and impact during the times when people are worried and struggling.*

While it's okay to express your concern—that's part of being vulnerable—people don't need to have your own fears imposed on them. They don't need to hear rumor and gossip. And they don't need an environment of increased stress and anxiety. What this partly translates into is simply staying off their backs, the opposite of what the old top-down managers will want to do.

Redefine Success

I recall an economic downturn that created a financial crisis in our company several years ago. The CEO called a meeting of all the senior executives, told us the extent of the problem, then allocated cost-cutting requirements for each of us. As president of the largest group, my assignment was to cut a million and a half dollars from the budget. I knew that other senior executives around the company intended to scour the individual departmental budgets, identify likely cuts, then impose them on the managers. It struck me that this was creating a lot of unnecessary anxiety among the employees and their managers, who could do nothing but wait to see what the boss wanted to cut.

I've always observed that when people are given a quota, they'll make sure they meet the quota and not one penny more. So rather than divvy up the million and a half dollars among the departments in my group, I called the senior managers together and said, "Okay, folks, we have to cut a million and a half dollars. Any ideas about how to do it?" People began volunteering to postpone expenditures to the following fiscal year, to cut their travel budgets, to cancel conferences, and to make small product adjustments. After a half hour or so, I knew we'd make the goal, so I said, "Okay, go back to your own operations, put a pencil to all these suggestions, then let me know by first thing tomorrow morning just how much each of you will commit to cut this fiscal year."

The next morning, they delivered their revised budgets. The total was almost three million dollars in savings. When I called the CEO and gave him the number, he was not only astounded but also very grateful for the financial cushion this would give him as he assembled his numbers for the board of directors.

"How did you do it?" he asked.

"I didn't do it," I replied. "I just asked my people to help, and this is what they came up with."

There are lessons here that go to the heart of servant leadership (a term which, at the time, I'd not even heard yet). First, my boss, the CEO, a servant leader himself, could have been cynical and said, "You guys must have padded your budget in the first place." Rather, he accepted that my people had stretched themselves and sacrificed to come up with the savings.

Next, my people could just as easily have thought along the same lines as the CEO: "Gee, if I come up with any substantial savings, Jim will think I padded the budget in the first place." But when the people know that you trust them and you're always willing to do what you can to be a resource for them, they will in turn respond when you ask for their help. What they achieved in this case was a triumph of skilled financial management, which we celebrated as a significant success despite the financial crisis.

There is another side to this coin as well. Just as depression and hysteria are not appropriate or realistic responses to a crisis, neither are bravado and bombast. During the early 2001 downturn, a manager in a media company issued a memo to his staff saying that he was just not going to accept that there was a downturn, that he was going to ignore it, and that the strategy he had developed for facing the gloomy advertising revenue forecast was to "sell right through it" and meet the original revenue goals for the company.

While we can admire his spirit, his way of expressing it was inappropriate for several reasons. Everyone in the company knew there was no way to make the revenue forecast, thus no one believed him. One employee told me, "His memo was silly. He may have managed to pump up his own morale, but it didn't work on me or on anyone I know. In fact, we think he set himself up to fail." The employee's insight was right on the button because, by rejecting the downturn and continuing to define the company's success as achieving the original revenue forecast, he had dismissed the possibility that there could be any other definition of success.

What he should have done was admit that the downturn was going to have an impact, then define success in another way. For instance, he might have asked for cost-cutting measures to protect the bottom line even with revenue shortfalls. Then he might have focused on share of market rather than total revenue, telling the people, "I'll consider that we've succeeded admirably if during this tough period we can maintain or perhaps even increase our share of market." These approaches would have given the people realistic goals and a constructive way to respond, plus it would have been good business management. What he did, however, only made the people realize they faced an impossible task and, by extension, fear that there may be negative consequences for not accomplishing the impossible.

Remember that there is no crisis that justifies the suspension of your servant leadership values and practices, one of which is open and honest communication in an environment of trust. So don't color the truth one way or the other; don't overplay or underplay the problem.

> *Remember that there is no crisis that justifies the suspension of your servant leadership values and practices, one of which is open and honest communication in an environment of trust.*

Stay Centered and Trust the People

There are times when the scope of a crisis may seem so large, when there are so many elements of such complexity that a commitment to focus leadership efforts on your employees seems the last thing on your agenda. Never give in to the temptation to put any other element or situation above the welfare of the people. Nothing is as important or is as likely to help your organization get through its crisis as the continued commitment and hard work of your people.

I've been through it time and again throughout the economic ups and downs of the past twenty years. There's nothing you can do to improve consumer confidence; there's nothing you can do about the Fed and its interest rate machinations; there's nothing you can do about currency evaluations or the balance of trade. And there's even very little you can do within your own industry or area of activity. Most of the time, the pattern is the same: cut costs, live as close to the bone as possible, increase your efforts to create satisfied customers, and realize that crisis time is sometimes the best time for innovation and new ideas. Nothing from the executive suite can make any of this happen; it all depends on the people.

Even when the circumstances seem far removed from the employees and the day-to-day operations, it's often true that the answers still lie with the people.

A few years ago I served on the board of large midwestern department store chain. The company was successful over the long-term and had been successful recently, but in the wake of a failed merchandising strategy, earnings fell for three quarters in a row. The stock price dropped to a new low.

As for the management team's response, it was thoughtful and focused. They moved quickly to change the merchandising approach, and even though such changes take time, the board was comfortable that the coming Christmas season would see an upturn in earnings followed by an increase in market evaluation.

But our optimism was cut short by a sudden hostile takeover bid. This, of course, is part of the peril that publicly held company executives face when the stock price falls even temporarily below what the company is actually worth. There are takeover artists just waiting to pounce. This was one of those times. (Though there are those who would argue that this aspect of our system only works to make companies stronger, I contend that this is a major weakness in the system and tends to create a bias toward short-term decisions and quarter-to-quarter management. Live quarter to quarter, die quarter to quarter.)

We were stunned by the maneuver but responded as a responsible board should. The offer was inadequate and we rejected it. There are also law firms waiting to pounce in these situations, so we were immediately slapped with stockholder suits.

Most people not familiar with these kinds of things would probably be shocked to find that all this is fairly normal and simply initiates a lengthy series of legal and financial maneuvers by both sides. I won't go into all that except to say that with stockholder meetings, potential election of hostile board members, and meetings with investment banking firms, attorneys and other assorted professionals, the management of the company is required to devote an inordinate amount of time to the process. To put it bluntly, it is a gigantic pain in the neck, and at the same time, it puts the company and its employees at considerable risk because all this can be so distracting that it creates enormous communications gaps and morale problems, both of which can work to only make matters worse. Not only that, the employees are bombarded with television and newspaper reports of the proceedings, the problem being that the news reports are not—and, because of federal disclosure rules, can never be—comprehensive or entirely accurate.

In fact, the takeover artists know that a hostile bid will often result in lower productivity, lower results, and lower earnings, which then provoke a lower stock price, which then makes the takeover bid price seem more attractive to the stockholders.

With all the disruption inherent in the situation, the management team and the board knew that the only way we could hold on and resist the takeover was with improved earnings results that might drive the stock price upward. We also knew that improving results would make the company more attractive to another, more friendly, and more compatible company. In fact, the CEO had been discussing mergers and acquisitions with other companies on a regular basis during the preceding year.

To review, this was truly a crisis of many dimensions. On the one hand, the greatest possible opportunity to fend off the hostile bid was to produce results, increase earnings, and hope the stock price also increased. On the other, the very chaos of the process was so preoccupying that it threatened to disrupt top management while distracting and confusing middle managers and employees. Furthermore, the CEO was under constant pressure to communicate with lawyers, accountants, and bankers, as well as the board, management team, employees, and community at large. This is not to mention the need to try to reassure stockholders, investors, and particularly Wall Street financial analysts upon whose opinion so much of a company's stock prospects depend.

Now, given the situation, can you guess which group most CEOs would concentrate on? If you said, "financial analysts," you'd be right. Most CEOs would put an extraordinary effort into jawboning with the analysts. Indeed, this CEO did put quite a bit of time and effort into it, but he also did something I've not seen any other CEO do: He spent even more time with the employees in the stores.

One day in the very thick of the situation, I asked him, "Tom, I'm concerned that you're taking care of yourself, so tell me how you're spending your day."

"Don't worry, Jim," he said. "Every morning I start the day by praying for about twenty minutes, then I meditate for twenty minutes."

"Are you asking the Almighty to pull us out of this situation?" I asked, somewhat in jest.

"No, just asking God to help me stay centered and focused on what's important."

"Then what do you do?"

"I go to the office and I walk around the store. I also call around to the other stores and travel to as many of them as I can, and every week on our TV network [a closed-circuit setup in all the stores], I talk to the employees."

"What's your message?"

"First I reassure them that we're doing all we can, and I explain within the limits of the law what's going on. Then I just tell them it's in their hands. I say, 'This company has always depended on you for its success. We in management made some merchandising errors last year, and now we're depending on you again for success. If we can increase our performance, we can beat this takeover and ensure the survival of our stores and our jobs.' Then I tell them I'm optimistic because I can do what I have to do, knowing that this is the best department store staff in the country. And I ask for questions and suggestions."

"Have you taken any of their suggestions?"

"You bet. Particularly on pricing."

"And are you optimistic?"

"I am. I think we'll increase our comp store sales this season, and we'll come into the new year with a good earnings report. Then we'll see what happens."

I then asked him about Wall Street and the analysts. "I do as much of that as I have to do," he said, "but those people only react, they don't proact. They can't win this for us. Our employees are the people who will make the difference, or we won't win."

Then he concluded, "And listen, too many retailers in this country have concentrated too much on Wall Street and not enough on Main Street."

I smiled and thought to myself, but didn't tell him at the time, we are going to win. And we did. The earnings improved, Tom found another company with whose CEO he'd been talking for several months, and they put together a deal from which everyone benefited—management, employees, and stockholders.

And P.S., that combined company a few years later acquired (without hostilities) the company that had made the original hostile takeover bid. Poetic justice.

Another thing Tom had done as part of his management approach was to treat his vendors like partners; in effect he became a servant leader to the people from whom the company bought its line of goods. Thus, during the crisis, the vendors really wanted to help and were generous with their discounts.

Tom explained his philosophy this way. "I've always tried to create an infinite circle of prosperity. To put it another way, I want a regenerative circle of prosperity that connects the customer with the associate with the shareholder with the vendor, so that all prosper. The customer gets value, quality, and service; the associate gets personal and financial rewards; the vendor gets a fair price for his goods and services; and the stockholder gets a fair return on investment."

I offer this concept of a "regenerative circle of prosperity" as an example of how one leader is able to manifest an attitude of servant leadership beyond those he directly leads, while at the same time creating a successful enterprise. I suggest this concept would apply to any kind of organization, and I suggest further that developing your own strong philosophical basis for organizational leadership is your most valuable asset in times of crisis.

Prepare Yourself and Your People

There's an old saying, "Don't expect the worst, but be prepared for it." For the leader, there are two basic kinds of preparation: institutional and personal.

The institutional preparations will vary from organization to organization, but generally these are the kinds of things you put in the "contingency" section of a strategic plan. They may involve cost cutting, plant closings, layoffs, and so on, each with a dollar savings amount attached. The major guideline in most organizations is to begin with the least painful cuts at the top of the list, then work downward as the situation dictates. I would add only that the servant leader should solicit the ideas of the employees in developing these contingencies.

(What I am not discussing here is "disaster planning," those procedures and responses in case of fire, flood, earthquake, or other disaster. I leave that discussion to your individual organizational policies and procedures.)

As for personal preparations, part of the evolution of a servant leader is in working to maintain the same attributes and characteristics in every situation. And how can you do that? How can you remain present, fully there, and deal with all the frustrations, stress and, yes, fear inherent in times of crisis?

An example from the martial arts may be helpful. Dr. Stuart Heller, who is known as "Dr. Move," is a sixth-degree black belt in two of the martial arts. He told me once that the key is remaining conscious and aware.

"In the face of fear and stress," he said, "our immediate instinct is to recoil, to become, as it is said, 'paralyzed by fear.' The master in the martial arts learns to remain conscious in the midst of danger, undistracted by what's going on around him, aware, and ready to respond."

Think about that. "Conscious in the midst of danger . . . aware, and ready to respond." Stuart made me realize that this is what the most accomplished people are able to do, whether mountain climbing, flying jet fighters, or any other risky enterprise—even, as my friend Tom did, fighting off a hostile takeover.

Just as leaders must see to their own psychological, emotional, and spiritual preparation, so too must they help their employees be prepared in the same way.

There is no better example of this than in Shakespeare's *Henry V*. One of the high points of the play is Henry's St. Crispin's Day speech to his troops before going into battle. As the scene opens, the generals are complaining that they don't have enough men to do the job, that the French have them outnumbered five to one. Then one of them says, "O that we now had here / But one ten thousand of those men in England / That do no work today." (act 4, scene 3)

The king overhears this conversation and interrupts. The king, of course, knows that there will be no reinforcements, no other resources beyond what they have with them at that time. What is he to do? What can he say to prepare them psychologically, emotionally, and spiritually?

To prevent this crisis from becoming a military disaster, he has to accomplish two major things, both of which you've already read in this book in one form or another: (1) He has to present a compelling vision and connect that vision with each soldier's vision of how life will be if he lives through this battle; (2) he has to build community, a sense that they're all in it together, including the king.

The king begins by reminding the group that tomorrow is the feast of St. Crispin, or St. Crispin's Day. He suggests that years from now, they will all remember tomorrow. Then he paints a picture of a future St. Crispin's Day feast as if each soldier has lived to old age and is hosting his neighbors. The old soldier, he says, will "strip his sleeve and show his scars, / And say 'These wounds I had on Crispin's Day.' / Old men . . . [will] remember, with advantages, / What feats [they] did that day."

Our names will be freshly remembered, he says, continuing the heroic picture, then he calls out the names of some of those listening to his speech as if they were being toasted at this feast of the future. At the high point of this scene, the morale has visibly risen, and he says the famous lines, "And Crispin Crispian shall ne'er go by / From this day to the ending of the world / But we in it shall be remembered. / We few, we happy few, we band of brothers— / For he today that sheds his blood with me / Shall be my brother . . . And gentlemen in England, now abed, / Shall think themselves accurs'd they were not here, / And hold their manhoods cheap whiles any speaks, / That fought with us upon St. Crispin's Day."

As a courier arrives to tell of the approach of the French, the king ends his speech with, "All things are ready, if our minds be so."

I frequently use a video of this speech in my leadership workshops, to demonstrate the power of language and its value as your most important leadership tool. And in times of crisis, it is sometimes the only tool you have.

What if you fail?

It won't make you feel any better if you get fired, but think about this: There's a great difference between recognizing that something you attempted failed, and feeling that you have failed. Yes, your work is important; yes, it helps give your life meaning and purpose; but it is not you, and you are not your work.

It's okay to be disappointed that a piece of your work failed. It's okay to feel devastated if you lose your job. These feelings are normal, and if they can lead you to examine the circumstances and learn from them, they can be positive.

But it's not okay to think of yourself as a failure. This is buying into the old winner-loser mentality that distorts so much of our activity, and it diminishes and devalues the experience of trying and failing, which sure beats not trying at all.

Once again, servant leadership requires courage and faith: courage to face everything that goes with failing or being fired, and faith that what you've learned will lead to better things in the future.

But I don't want to sound like your old uncle trying to buck you up to face the future. It's no fun to see something or someone you've put your very soul into fail to meet your expectations, and it's certainly no fun to lose a job with all the financial and identity crises that can result.

Yet it is in these times of crisis and failure that the characteristics of servant leadership, detailed in chapter 1, come into play as your greatest support. They will take you through the bad times and into better ones, no matter how bad the times may get.

So be authentic, be your real self at all times. Be vulnerable. Don't act as if bad times don't hurt or don't affect you intensely. Admitting that, and living through it, is vital. Be accepting. Of bad situations as well as good, of failure as well as success. Be present. To all the possibilities for the future, to those around you who may be suffering and who have not yet developed the emotional strength you have. And, by all means, be useful. Be of service to yourself, to your family, to anyone else who may be affected negatively by the crisis at hand.

And if I may add to the words of Shakespeare, remember that "All things are ready, if our minds [and spirits] be so."

Script for a Future Slide Show

WHEN I SPEAK ON the subjects of servant leadership, bringing your spirit to work, and the "caring workplace," it is inevitable that someone, after pointing out that we don't live in a perfect world, usually questions my grip on reality and asks what I'm trying to prove anyway.

What I'm trying to prove is that there is a better way to be in organizational life, a way that will produce more of every kind of reward—emotional, psychological, spiritual, and financial—for everyone involved, employees, managers, the owners (stockholders), and the society. I do not succeed all the time, but I regularly take this message to organizations and try to help their managers and leaders inculcate these ideas into their own operations. Sometimes the message falls on deaf ears, but most of the time I succeed in getting a majority of the managers to at least try what I teach.

As for my own experience in a senior executive role, the ten-year business record of the group of which I was president is clear, and I believe that by any factor—measurable or intuitive—the employees and managers felt and appreciated the differences I tried to make.

But by no means was I able to accomplish the perfect workplace. That, on the face of it, is an impossibility because there will always be a higher standard to achieve, if for no other reasons than the reality of people's expectations and their capacity to grow. So I can't define an impossibility, but I can get close to how I would like to see all organizations be sometime soon.

Based on the principles in this book, I can envision the new American workplace created by servant leaders, and I'd like to try to show you what it looks like. I think I can do that by resorting to what admittedly is sort of a corny gimmick: pretending I was sent for one day in the year 2015 to visit several organizations, and that I was allowed to take my camera along. Now, if you want to see how things could be fifteen years from now, what you have to do is pretend that you are in my living room watching the resulting slide show. I apologize in advance for not being up-to-date and giving a PowerPoint presentation, but I still like the old slide projector. And I apologize also for having no real photographs to show you; I ask that you read the script and use your imagination.

Slide 1

Here's a shot of a parking lot. Looks like a thousand other parking lots outside of big buildings. But notice that, except for a section for employees with disabilities, there are no signs with names on them, no signs with color codes, and no other special sections. No elitism in this parking lot. It's first come, first served. Apparently the leaders here, to their credit, can do without the ego boost of an executive parking space.

Slide 2

Here's a shot in the office of the organization's chief executive. It's small but adequate for a meeting area as well as a desk. Lots of personal stuff, plus a computer, fax, PDA, and some other high-tech gadgets any chief executive needs in the year 2015.

Slide 3

Now this one is interesting. It's of another office. Looks about the same in size, perhaps a little smaller, but not noticeably. It's the office of one of the lower-level salespeople. I asked about its similarity to the boss's office. Seems that everyone gets an office of about the same size, the differences being determined only by function and need. For instance, the president needs a meeting area; a graphic designer needs a drawing board; and a salesperson needs only a desk and phone and files. Every employee's office starts out essentially as a white box. The employee is given a budget and advice in decorating; thus every office is very personal, with people surrounded by the things that mean the most to them and which contribute most to their sense of comfort and well-being. The theory is that, in such a personalized setting, the employee will do better, more productive, more creative work. I wasn't able to stay long enough to find out, but it makes sense to me.

Slide 4

This one looks like any typical meeting, but see the woman in the center? She's the manager, and the others are her employees. If you look closely, you can see that she is holding a form. That's her employee evaluation form. I don't mean the form by which she evaluates the employees, but the other way around. She's looking at the form that represents the consensus of her employees' evaluations of her. This is a once-a-year event; I was lucky to be there on that very day. As you can see, no one is laughing, although I can tell you there was a lot of goodwill and respect in the room that day. The process, it seems, is made all the more important by the fact that the employee evaluation becomes part of the manager's record and is considered by her boss as part of the annual performance standards review.

After taking this shot, I asked if all this didn't put the manager in the position of trying constantly to win a popularity contest and if so, didn't that undermine the manager's effectiveness in doing the hard tasks of discipline and termination? Surprisingly, the answer was to the contrary of what I might have expected. Many times, the employees criticize the boss for not doing those hard discipline jobs. And come to think of it, those are the jobs that most often get ignored or postponed.

Slide 5

Now here's one of my favorite shots. I took it at a party given for an employee who was receiving an Excellence Award, in recognition of a highly productive month in the mail-opening department. He's the guy looking at the camera, the one standing to the right of the woman in the wheelchair. Yeah, that's right, the funny-looking guy with his hand up to his mouth. You see, I found out that he has autism, and while he does terrific work, he can't take a lot of excitement. It seems that when he get stressed out, he bites the back of his hand. I was told that at first, a lot of the employees were put off by what they thought was pretty goofy behavior. Some of them were even scared. But then they discovered he only bit his own hand, and while it seemed a bit self-destructive, it was no more so than ducking out for a relaxing cigarette or having a drink after work. Also, it didn't take long to realize that he had such an awesome power of concentration, his work was unparalleled by anyone else, even the people who had been at it a long time.

Slide 6

This scene is not so happy. The woman on the left is one of the company counselors, a licensed clinical psychologist, I believe, and the man and woman on the right are an employee and her husband. Obviously, it would have been inappropriate for me to do more than snap my shot and leave, so I don't know what they were discussing, but you can see it was serious. I do know that family counselors and psychotherapists are available, even after office hours, for counseling and referral services, to help any employee who has a problem. The sessions are completely confidential, and the names of the employees who use the services are confidential and never appear in any file except the counselors'. Another thing, I found out the counseling department, called "employee assistance" in some places, reports directly to the CEO.

Slide 7

Back to a happier note, I took this shot as performance-based bonuses were being announced in this department. The stuff on the floor is confetti someone threw at the department head after he gave them the news. As I left, they were making up some kind of cheer about doing even better next year.

Slide 8

This looks like a regular meeting, the kind you see every day in your own organization, but this is a peer review session. See the man in the blue shirt with the floral tie? He's being reviewed by a group of his peers, people at his same general job level who are doing the same general kinds of work. In this case, they're all mid-level managers, the most difficult management spot in any company. The man is looking a bit perplexed in this shot; he's just been told that his style is too blunt and directive, that he needs to improve his listening skills. It seems that some of his peers had been approached for job opportunities by some of his people. A bad sign. I understand that he'll be given a copy of this critique and will be given an opportunity to respond. I understand also that this does not become a part of his record and is not given to his manager or to the HR department. This is considered to be a collegial approach to critique and review, an informal process. You could call it sort of a support group.

Slide 9

And speaking of support groups, I took this picture during a luncheon meeting of a twelve-step group. This idea is based on the approach used by Alcoholics Anonymous, only this group is not limited to people with any specific problem. When I explained that I have been in twelve-step groups myself and know the protocol and the guarantees of privacy, they invited me to stay for this session. Some of the people had substance abuse problems, others had marital problems, others simply had compulsive behaviors they wanted to overcome, such as gambling or overeating or smoking. (Yes, they'll still be smoking in 2015.) I learned that there were several of these groups, which met at the company's facilities, but during the off-hours, even on weekends. As I'm sure most of you know, the churches and social service organizations have provided most of the support for these twelve-step groups in years past, but in 2015, many of them meet at the very place that causes much of the stress: the workplace.

Slide 10

Here's another lunchtime activity, an aerobics class. Nothing new here; a lot of this was going on in 2000 and before, but there's a difference. In 2015 many companies have taken innovative steps to hold down medical costs. Employees have to pay part of the bill, as they did in 2000, but employees who participate on their own time in fitness and stress management and relaxation programs are given a discount on their share of the premiums. Several organizations are doing longitudinal studies to determine the cost effectiveness of this approach. Whether it significantly cuts health-care costs or not, it still struck me as a good investment in morale and productivity.

Slide 11

More of the same. Only this is a meditation and guided imagery class. The guy you see in the corner, with the little black box, is doing biofeedback to lower his respiration and blood pressure rates. I was told he used to have daily headaches and beat them with relaxation exercises and biofeedback. Organizations all over the country report that the employees who participate in these programs have fewer health-care claims, thus are more productive. Not to mention a lot happier with themselves and with everyone around them.

Slide 12

Back to a party scene. This time it's a retirement, but there's a difference. The man you see here is retiring, to be sure; but as part of a special program, he told the company six months ago that he'd like to continue some kind of work, not for the money but because he felt he still had a lot to contribute. This is an old problem, of course, but apparently in 2015, they're doing something about it. This man will now become the company's representative to a social service organization or a volunteer health agency or other charitable group. The company will pay travel and living expenses when he's doing these duties, but no salary. It's a great win-win idea: he gets productive and important work to do; the company gets to be well represented and to further extend its influence as a caring company; and the organization gets a highly qualified volunteer. All the laughter you see was in response to his wife's comment that it'll also get him out of the house and out of her way once in awhile. This retirement party certainly did not seem like the kind of funereal gatherings so prevalent in 1990 and 2000.

Slide 13

Here's another meeting. I know a lot of these photographs look the same, and I apologize for that, but on the surface one meeting looks like another. It's what's going on in the meeting that counts. This one happens to be a meeting of the Termination Review Board. Every firing is reviewed with the managers involved. The history of performance appraisals is reviewed; the records of conversations and memos are studied; the steps taken to correct the situation are retraced; and the severance and outplacement arrangements are evaluated. Obviously an employee can fail, but the attitude at this company was that management still must examine what could have been done to prevent the failure. So every firing is considered serious enough to require a review somewhat like those of the medical profession in reviewing case management or surgical procedures. Makes sense to me. After all, being fired can change a person's life as drastically as many surgeries.

Slide 14

An empty desk. It may seem like a strange picture, but this is the desk of a man who was home, on parental leave, with his wife during the first week of their new baby's life. He was being paid full salary for the first three weeks, then would be free to take unpaid leave— all this with no negative impact on his regular vacation benefits.

Slide 15

And this picture is of a woman just back from another kind of leave, an educational leave. The woman shaking her hand is the CEO of one of the organizations I visited. The framed document between them is the younger woman's MBA, which she earned during a leave of absence, with pay. She paid her own tuition, but the company continued her salary and benefits. I was particularly impressed with this program, which, it seemed to me, worked both for the company and for the employees.

Back in 1998, the CEO of this company realized that there would have been a critical shortage of bright, educated people within a very few years. So in addition to the regular tuition aid program, which most companies had at the time, she established an Advanced Education Program.

It works like this: After an employee has completed a certain number of hours toward a graduate degree, using the regular tuition aid program and personal time, the employee can apply for Advanced Education leave. The field of study must be one that the company determines will advance knowledge and skills needed for the future of the company. If granted, the employee can attend the educational institution of choice. In return, the employee agrees to return to the company for a specified number of years. In this woman's case, she has agreed to stay for twice the amount of time she was on leave. She told me, right after I snapped the shutter, that she didn't plan to ever leave.

Slides 16–24

I used the last nine shots to record these random photos of people at their jobs. I just walked around and shot these before I left. Nothing unusual really, just people at their jobs—but there is one thing I should point out: These people were working on a special project that day and had agreed among themselves to work until it was done. I took all these shots two hours after quitting time when everyone was supposed to be gone for the day! This just seemed the perfect thing to end my slide show.

Thank you for sitting through all this. I know how tiring watching someone else's slides can be, but at least you can be thankful I had an old-fashioned camera and only one twenty-four-exposure roll of film.

Index